Powerful Transformation

The Alchemy of the *Secret Heart Essence*

RANGJUNG YESHE BOOKS • www.rangjung.com

PADMASAMBHAVA: *Treasures from Juniper Ridge* • *Advice from the Lotus-Born* • *Dakini Teachings* • *Following in Your Footsteps: The Lotus-Born Guru in Nepal* • *Following in Your Footsteps: The Lotus-Born Guru in India*

PADMASAMBHAVA AND JAMGÖN KONGTRÜL:
The Light of Wisdom, Vol. 1, Vol. 2, Vol. 3, Secret, Vol. 4 & Vol. 5

PADMASAMBHAVA, CHOKGYUR LINGPA, JAMYANG KHYENTSE WANGPO,
TULKU URGYEN RINPOCHE, ORGYEN TOBGYAL RINPOCHE, & OTHERS
Dispeller of Obstacles • *The Tara Compendium* • *Powerful Transformation* • *Dakini Activity*

YESHE TSOGYAL: *The Lotus-Born*

DAKPO TASHI NAMGYAL: *Clarifying the Natural State*

TSELE NATSOK RANGDRÖL: *Mirror of Mindfulness* • *Heart Lamp* • *Empowerment and Samaya*

CHOKGYUR LINGPA: *Ocean of Amrita* • *The Great Gate* • *Skillful Grace* • *Great Accomplishment* • *Guru Heart Practices*

TRAKTUNG DUDJOM LINGPA: *A Clear Mirror*

JAMGÖN MIPHAM RINPOCHE: *Gateway to Knowledge, Vol. 1, Vol. 2, Vol. 3 & Vol. 4*

TULKU URGYEN RINPOCHE: *Blazing Splendor* • *Rainbow Painting* • *As It Is, Vol. 1 & Vol. 2* • *Vajra Speech* • *Repeating the Words of the Buddha* • *Dzogchen Deity Practice* • *Vajra Heart Revisited*

ADEU RINPOCHE: *Freedom in Bondage*

KHENCHEN THRANGU RINPOCHE: *Crystal Clear* • *Songs of True Accomplishment*

CHÖKYI NYIMA RINPOCHE: *Bardo Guidebook* • *Collected Works of Chökyi Nyima Rinpoche, Vol. 1 & Vol. 2*

TULKU THONDUP: *Enlightened Living*

ORGYEN TOBGYAL RINPOCHE: *Life & Teachings of Chokgyur Lingpa* • *Straight Talk* • *Sublime Lady of Immortality*

DZIGAR KONGTRÜL RINPOCHE: *Uncommon Happiness*

TSOKNYI RINPOCHE: *Fearless Simplicity* • *Carefree Dignity*

MARCIA DECHEN WANGMO: *Dzogchen Primer* • *Dzogchen Essentials* • *Quintessential Dzogchen* • *Confessions of a Gypsy Yogini* • *Precious Songs of Awakening Compilation*

ERIK PEMA KUNSANG: *Wellsprings of the Great Perfection* • *A Tibetan Buddhist Companion* • *The Rangjung Yeshe Tibetan-English Dictionary of Buddhist Culture & Perfect Clarity*

CHOKGYUR LINGPA, JAMGÖN KONGTRÜL, JAMYANG KHYENTSE WANGPO,
ADEU RINPOCHE, AND ORGYEN TOPGYAL RINPOCHE • *The Tara Compendium Feminine Principles Discovered*

Powerful Transformation

The Alchemy of the *Secret Heart Essence*

Chokgyur Lingpa
Dilgo Khyentse Rinpoche
Do Khyentse Yeshe Dorje
Karmapa Khakyab Dorje
Karmey Khenpo Rinchen Dargye
Künzang Gyurmey Tsewang Drakpa
Orgyen Tobgyal Rinpoche
Padma Garwang Dorje Tsal
Padmasambhava
Pema Drimé Lodrö Shyenpen Chökyi Nangwa
Terdok Lingpa
Tsikey Chokling Rinpoche
Tulku Urgyen Rinpoche

PUBLICATIONS

Rangjung Yeshe Publications
526 Entrada Drive, Apt. 201
Novato, CA 94949 USA

Address letters to:
Rangjung Yeshe Publications
C/O Above

www.rangjung.com
www.lotustreasure.com

Copyright© 2017–2025 Rangjung Yeshe Publications, except *Daily Practice of Vajrasattva*, Mindroling Dorsem© Shechen Publications.

All rights reserved. No part of this book may be reproduced in any form or by any means, electronic or mechanical—including photocopying, recording, and duplicating by means of any information storage and retrieval system—without written permission from the publisher.

First paperback edition published in 2017

Printed in the United States of America

Publication data: ISBN-13: 978-0-9977162-0-7 (pbk)

Title: POWERFUL TRANSFORMATION: The Alchemy of the *Secret Heart Essence*
Chokgyur Lingpa, Dilgo Khyentse Rinpoche, Do Khyentse Yeshe Dorje, Karmapa Khakyab Dorje, Karmey Khenpo Rinchen Dargye, Künzang Gyurmey Tsewang Drakpa, Orgyen Tobgyal Rinpoche, Padma Garwang Dorje Tsal, Padmasambhava, Pema Drimé Lodrö Shyenpen Chökyi Nangwa, Terdok Lingpa, Tsikey Chokling Rinpoche, Tulku Urgyen Rinpoche

1. Vajrayana/Yidam—Tradition of Pith Instructions
2. Buddhism—Tibet

Photos courtesy of Graham Sunstein & Marcia Binder Schmidt

Cover Art by Maryann Lipaj

FIRST EDITION

Contents

Preface *Marcia Binder Schmidt*	1
Overview of Yidam Practice *Tulku Urgyen Rinpoche*	5

Vajrakilaya Practice

Introduction to Sangtik Phurba *Tsikey Chokling Rinpoche*	17
Sangtik Phurba Lineage Supplication *Künzang Gyurmey Tsewang Drakpa*	21
The Sadhana of the Single Form of Vajrakumara *Chokgyur Lingpa*	23
A Roar to Delight Heruka *Karmey Khenpo Rinchen Dargye*	39
Clarifying Notes for the Sadhana of Vajrakilaya *Kyabje Dilgo Khyentse Rinpoche*	61
The Practice of the Single Form of Vajrakilaya *Orgyen Tobgyal Rinpoche*	75

Vajrasattva Practice

The Aspiration of Vajrasattva EXTRACTED FROM *Vajrasattva's Root Tantra Heart Bindu*	107
Essence of Blessings *The Fifteenth Karmapa, Khakyab Dorje*	109
The Practice of the Single Form of Vajrasattva *Chokgyur Lingpa*	111
The Words of Vajrasattva *Pema Drimé Lodrö Shyenpen Chökyi Nangwa*	119

Contents

Practicing in an Absolute Way   141
Tulku Urgyen Rinpoche

ADDITIONAL WAYS TO PRACTICE VAJRASATTVA

The Visualization and Recitation of Vajrasattva   147
Chokgyur Lingpa

Vajrasattva Preliminaries   151
Tulku Urgyen Rinpoche

Abridged Daily Practice of Vajrasattva   165
ADAPTED BY *Kyabje Dilgo Khyentse Rinpoche*

Commentary on Abridged Daily Practice
of Vajrasattva   169
Tulku Urgyen Rinpoche

Daily Practice of Vajrasattva   191
EXTRACTED BY *Padma Garwang Dorje Tsal*

Vajrasattva Drubchen   201
Orgyen Tobgyal Rinpoche

The Heart of Vajrasattva   215
Do Khyentse Yeshe Dorje

Appendix, Extracted from
The Light of Wisdom, Volume II   217
*Padmasambhava, Chokgyur Lingpa,
Jamgön Kongtrül, and Jokyab Rinpoches*

Tibetan Source Material   221

Endnotes   223

Neten Phurba

Preface

Marcia Binder Schmidt

Powerful Transformation is the fourth book in the series of the Three Roots practices of lama, yidam, and dakini. Here, the two main deities are Vajrakilaya and Vajrasattva, who are considered both lama and yidam figures; and in Vajrakilaya's case, he's also a protector.

What exactly are powerful transformations and the alchemy of the *Heart Essence?* These are dynamics opened up by the elements of development and completion stage practices, applied in a sublime manner. Our misdeeds, obscurations, and habitual patterns prevent meditation experiences and realization from arising. Vajrasattva practice can purify these. When a yogi attains accomplishment, the obstacles become greater and can be overcome by Vajrakilaya practice, combined with recognition of mind's nature. In the *Secret Heart Essence,* these two powerful yidams are displayed as conduits to realization and accomplishment.

Alchemy only works if the pure properties are inherent to the material that needs to be altered. We do possess the enlightened essence; it is our core makeup. We have not fully connected to that, yet we can clear away the temporary obscurations that are impeding us. Although we aspire to fully actualizing our buddha nature and stabilizing our realization, we are continuously blocked from doing so by veils of negative emotions, past karma, and habitual tendencies. The substances that can clear these away and establish us in an accomplished state are deity, mantra, and samadhi, the key elements of the development and completion stages. Through meeting with an authentic lineage master, we can receive the instructions that will enable us to purify our stains and increase our merit enough to begin to practice. Eventually, we can reach the level of experiencing the wisdom of what we are practicing.

Moreover, there are certain negative conditions or obstacles that can prevent us from even being able to engage in the deity trainings. These of course include the outer, inner, and secret obstacles as well as the four maras: the aggregates, the conflicting emotions, the lord of death, and the son of the gods. Faced with these seemingly insurmountable hindrances, we are amazingly fortunate to even seek the dharma—both teacher and teachings. Yet, somehow, our innate awareness keeps calling out to us to do so and to move beyond any constraints that our various obstructions impose upon us. Hence, we connect with Vajrakilaya and Vajrasattva, two of the most formidable, sublime beings to initiate change and engender strength and purity.

There are many levels to practicing deity yoga, according to individual capability. We can unfold the sadhana from within the view of the Dzogchen or build it within the framework of the more gradual elements of the traditional development and completion stages. But what really matters is finding the most expedient way to realize the wisdom mind of whichever deity we are practicing and transforming our ordinary grasping and fixation into experience. So how we go about that is a key point. Also, depending on our proclivities, we choose either peaceful or wrathful yidams to work with our strongest conflicting emotions. This is the alchemy that changes our coarse realities and brings us closer to seeing things as they truly are. The skillful methods of Vajrayana are the conduits for clearing away the veils that hinder our ability to actualize all-encompassing purity. Right now, most of us need to imitate this underlying principle when we train in sadhana practice. Eventually, we will have intergrated it into our stream of being.

Teachings on various ways to practice these hidden treasures of Chokgyur Lingpa include commentaries by Karmey Khenpo Rinchen Dargye, Kyabje Dilgo Khyentse Rinpoche, Tulku Urgyen Rinpoche, Tsikey Chokling Rinpoche, Orgyen Tobgyal Rinpoche, and others. There are various styles that we can apply, depending on our natural inclinations and trainings. The first half of the book describes the practice of Vajrakilaya in great detail, and the second half gives explanations on Vajrasattva. Included are different practices of Vajrasattva, be it the preliminaries, daily practice, or drubchen.

Many talented people have come together to work on this book. They include the many translators: Erik Pema Kunsang, Bo Colomby,

Matthieu Ricard, Lama Sean Price, Ryan Conlon, and Ani Laura Dainty. Thanks to all of them for their gifted generosity and diligence, working in some cases with very difficult original texts. Then there is the keen and clear-eyed editor, Anne Paniagua; the consistent book designer, Joan Olson; the multi-talented cover designer, Maryann Lipaj; and the wonderful proofreaders, Lynn Shroeder and Michael Yockey, and the kind sponsorship from the Gere Foundation. None of this could be completed without any one of them.

Here is where I make a heartfelt offering and aspiration to benefit the dharma, fulfill the wishes of my teachers, and clear away obstacles so practitioners can accomplish purification and ultimate enlightenment. If there are any errors in this endeavor, I take full responsibility for them. Forgive such mistakes and please take these extraordinary teachings to heart and apply them. Leaving mere words on the pages of a book, though virtuous, pales in comparison to practicing and realizing them. May all be auspicious!

Overview of Yidam Practice

Tulku Urgyen Rinpoche

In Tibetan, we refer to Dorje Phurba or Dorje Shonnu; in Sanskrit, his name is Vajrakilaya or Vajrakumara. All the victorious ones have [enlightened] body, speech, mind, qualities, and activities. The condensation of all the activities is Karma Heruka. For example, Amoghasiddhi represents one of the five families of the victorious ones. When Amoghasiddhi emanates in an extremely wrathful form, he is known as Karma Heruka, who accomplishes wrathful activity. When Karma Heruka further emanates in an even more wrathful form to tame the wild and untamable, he is called Dorje Phurba, Vajrakilaya. Primarily, he enacts the four activities: peaceful, increasing, magnetizing, and subjugating. However, Vajrakilaya also perfects the supreme activity, and everything is included within this.

Many of the Indian panditas attained accomplishment [practicing] Dorje Phurba. In the snowy land of Tibet, many became realized based on Phurba. The Nyingma lineage has three main wrathful deities: Mamo, Shinje, and Phurba. In Tibet, these three—Ma, Shin, Phur—are considered "the fence of the Dharma," which is extremely important. Ma, Shin, and Phur protect the doctrine, and if the practices of these three slip, especially that of Shinje, that will ultimately be the main cause for degeneration of the Dharma. Amongst these three, there are very few accomplished practitioners of Shinje and Phurba, and Shinje siddhas are the most rare. Regarding Shinje practice, I once asked Kyungtrul Rinpoche, our root guru, "Why will the doctrine in Tibet degenerate?" He answered, "Because there are not many accomplished Shinje practitioners. If there are not many siddhas of both Shinje and Phurba, the fence of the Tibetan Dharma collapses, and negative influences can enter." That is what the old lama said.

He also said, "Now times are peaceful, but there are foreboding signs that the doctrine in Tibet will decline. There used to be many Shinje siddhas before, but I do not hear of so many these days. What keeps the fence of the Dharma strong are these three, Ma, Shin, and Phurba. Without these, there will be degeneration. Before in each district, there were practitioners of Shinje; not so much anymore."

Vajrakilaya is the single form that embodies all buddha activity in an extremely wrathful way, and he can grant both the common and supreme accomplishments. Through practicing Phurba, we can attain realization of the wisdom deity and capture the dharmakaya throne within this lifetime—that is how great Phurba is. In essence, Vajrakilaya is not other than Samantabhadra, because the identity is Samantabhadra. The way of appearing is as the five buddha families, and the manifestations are the buddhas of the six realms. The identity or essence of any deity is not other than Buddha Samantabhadra.

. . .

Guru Rinpoche stayed at the Asura and Yangleshö caves in Nepal, where he attained accomplishment of both Yangdak and Phurba. His ultimate yidam was Yangdak, and the essence of Yangdak is Vajrasattva, whose wrathful emanation is Yangdak Heruka. At the time of attaining accomplishments, obstacles become greater and greater. Accomplishments are attained based on Yangdak and obstacles are cleared away by means of Phurba.

First, Guru Rinpoche attained supreme accomplishment by means of Yangdak. To overcome the obstacles, he sent [to India] for the Phurba text. As soon as the text arrived, the obstacles were overcome. He didn't even have to engage in the practice; the arrival of the text was enough.

Dudjom Rinpoche said that Bodhgaya is the place where the Buddha attained complete and perfect enlightenment. It is one of the most blessed places on this earth. For us, the place where Guru Rinpoche realized Yangdak is incredibly special, and there is no difference in blessings between Yangleshö and Bodhgaya. This place is like a second Bodhgaya.

Unfortunately, for us practitioners, there are definitely obstacles, and generally speaking there are three kinds: outer or external, inner, and innermost. External obstacles are imbalances in the outer elements, which manifest as natural disasters like earthquakes, floods, fires, and hurricanes. These create a lot of obvious difficulties for sentient beings.

Inner obstacles are imbalances in the nadis, pranas, and bindus—the channels, energies, and essences, also called the structuring channels, the moving winds, and the arrayed essences. These can be disturbed in various ways. The channels can be constricted, the winds or energies can be reversed and move in the wrong way, and the essences can be deranged. *Essence* here means mainly the white and red elements obtained from the father and mother. These three serve as the blueprint, the basic structure, for the human body. When they suffer from imbalances, we feel that our illusory physical body is sick. Of course, there are certain remedies we can use to cure such imbalances.

Most considerable of the obstacles, though, are the innermost ones, which involve fixating on perceiver and perceived. Basically, this refers to our habit of dualistic experience, which is caused by lack of stability in the original basic state of empty cognizance. When this empty cognizance is not stable in itself, its expression is to reach out and fixate on the five objects of experience—the five sense objects. They are the perceived. The perceiver is the mind that fixates upon them.

Although this basic, original state of self-existing wakefulness has no duality whatsoever, because we fixate upon experiences as being something other, "seeming duality" takes place. As it continues, this perpetuation of dualistic experience is exactly what characterizes the minds of all sentient beings. The minds of sentient beings are caught up in fixating on perceiver and perceived. This is the very core of samsaric existence, and this is in itself our innermost obstacle.

No one is beyond obstacles. We are all hurt and injured again and again by these three levels of obstacles. We can deal with external obstacles, the calamities of the four elements, by either moving to some other place or performing certain practices to appease, or pacify, the elemental forces.

The inner obstacles, imbalances in the vajra body's channels, energies, and essences, show themselves in physical sickness as well as various other ways. We can take medicine to treat these, as well as perform yogic exercises to control, manipulate, and master the movement of the energies in the channels and the placement of the essences. Such practices belong mainly to Mahayoga and Anuyoga, but Atiyoga has some aspects concerning this as well.

The most important point, though, is how to overcome the innermost obstacle of dualistic experience, the habit of holding on to perceiver and perceived. The only way to conquer that duality is to not let the expression stray into being dualistic mind, which apprehends duality where no duality exists. It is said, "Until duality dissolves into oneness, there is no enlightenment." We therefore need to acknowledge the nondual state of *rangjung yeshe*, the self-existing wakefulness that is our original state. After acknowledging it, we need to train in that and become stable. It is only through such stability that we can become totally victorious over all obstacles.

We furthermore need to overcome the power of the four maras, the four demons. Almost everyone is under their power, as only a few of us have actually managed to overcome all four maras at once. As a matter of fact, we are really only out of their grip when attaining rainbow body. Otherwise, whenever there is a corpse left behind, it means we didn't overcome the mara of the aggregates. It is very rare that someone can be free of all four. But, actually, Vajrakilaya himself is the deity that has conquered all four maras at once. So this is the main deity that all the great masters of the past practiced. This is their main yidam to reach accomplishment.

If you train in just one deity, like Vajrakilaya, practicing it first within the structure of the three samadis and then while recognizing mind essence, I can guarantee that within this one lifetime, you can accomplish both the common and supreme siddhis, the supreme siddhi of complete enlightenment.

Of the seven cycles of *Sangtik*, Chokling revealed *Yangdak*, *Vajrasattva*, and *Phurba*, and Jamgön Kongtrül[i] revealed the others. The whole sadhana of *Sangtik Phurba* is actually a visualization. The words mean something, and you should bring that to mind; saying it slowly, let the meaning of the words take hold before going to the next sentence. That is the whole idea of saying it in the first place. The commentarial instructions on the deity provide many details, but actually, if you just follow what it says here, line by line, trying to picture that, and then go to the next line, it is pretty complete as it is. You won't need to have a lot of details.

Practice in a simple way like this: First, remind yourself of being the deity, thinking, "I am Vajrakilaya." Then, recite the mantra, OM BENZA KILI KILAYA, or simply OM AH HUNG. Next, recognize that the one who imagines the deity and chants the mantra is none other than your own mind.

Without this mind, you could not visualize the form of the deity. Without mind, you could not chant the mantra. When you examine what it is that imagines or recites, recognizing your own mind, you see that it is an indivisible, empty cognizance, and not in some roundabout way. For example, if you want to touch space with your finger, how far do you need to move your finger in order to touch space? Doesn't it touch it the moment you first stretch your finger out? In the same way, the moment you recognize, you come in contact with the completion stage—the empty and cognizant nature of mind. You recognize it immediately. Thus, while seeing the nature of mind, you can carry on chanting the mantra.

When beginning your practice session, don't neglect to imagine the form of the deity. Without looking in the mirror, the face is not seen. Visualizing the deity means the mind mirror is allowed to think, "I am Vajrakilaya." It is all right to remind yourself that you are the deity, because your five aggregates and five elements from the very beginning are the mandala of buddhas.

In this way, by using the single thought, "I am the deity," visualization takes no more than an instant. This instantaneous recollection, bringing the deity vividly to mind in an instant, is the highest and best form of visualization. With your voice, chant the mantra, and with your mind, recognize. It is perfectly all right to decide that this type of practice is sufficient and all-inclusive. It's not like we have to please the wisdom deity, which has no thoughts anyway. Wisdom deities don't get pleased or displeased, so it is really more a matter of making up your own mind and practicing in this simple, all-inclusive way. This is my opinion. Maybe I'm being too simple here. On the other hand, maybe it is true.

The wisdom deity represents what is called *rangjung yeshe* in Tibetan, or *swayambhu jnana* in Sanskrit: self-existing wakefulness. In this way, the wisdom deity is indivisible from the nature of our own mind. The wisdom deity has no thoughts, and thus doesn't discriminate and is not pleased or displeased by our actions. However, a text cites, "Although the wisdom deity holds no thoughts, still, its oath-bound retinue sees the faults of people." While the wisdom deity itself is not made happy by offerings or unhappy if we forget, its total realization acts like a magnet to attract all sorts of mundane spirits. These mundane spirits do have shortcomings, they do have thoughts, and they do see the faults of people. They can either help or harm. The retinue of wisdom deities includes the *mamos,* the *tsen,* the *dü,* and all the different earth, fire, and water gods. Whether we make offerings or not does make a difference to them, but for wisdom deities themselves, it makes no difference, because they have no thoughts.

To reiterate, and this applies to the Vajrasattva practice as well, carry out whichever yidam practice you are involved in, practicing it within the structure of the three samadhis and while recognizing mind essence. If you practice like that, I can guarantee that within this one lifetime, you can accomplish both the common siddhis and the supreme siddhi of complete enlightenment.

Let me tell you a story to illustrate this. Sakya Pandita was not only an extremely learned master, but he was accomplished as well. He had developed clairvoyance based on sound. Traveling through a place along the Tibetan border, he listened to a stream running down the mountain. Through the water he heard the mantra of Vajrakilaya mispronounced OM BENZA CHILI CHILAYA SARVA BIGHANAM BAM HUNG PHAT. He thought, "Someone must be saying the wrong mantra up in the mountains; I'd better go up and correct him." He went up there and found this insignificant little meditation hut with a lama sitting inside. Sakya Pandita asked his name and what he was doing, and the lama replied, "My yidam is Vajrakilaya and that is what I'm doing." Sakya Pandita asked, "What mantra are you using?" and the lama said, "OM BENZA CHILI CHILAYA SARVA BIGHANAM BAM HUNG PHAT." Sakya Pandita said, "Oh, no! That's the wrong mantra; it's supposed to begin with OM BENZA KILI KILAYA. That's where the real meaning lies, in the words, 'Vajrakilaya with consort, the ten sons, and all the devourers and slayers.' They are contained within the sounds of the mantra." The meditator replied, "No, no, the words are not as important as the state of mind. Pure mind is more important than pure sound. I said CHILI CHILAYA in the past and that's what I will continue to say in the future. No doubt about that! You, on the other hand, will need my phurba." And the meditator gave Sakya Pandita his kilaya dagger, saying, "You take this with you." So he did.

Some time later, in Kyirong, which is on the Tibet-Nepal border, Sakya Pandita met with Shangkara, a Hindu master who wanted to convert the Tibetans. The two had a big debate, with the winner of each round getting one parasol or umbrella as a symbol of his victory. Each had won nine, and there was one left. At that point, Shangkara flew up into the sky, as a magical display of his siddhis. While he was levitating there, Sakya Pandita took his dagger and chanted, "OM BENZA CHILI CHILAYA..." Shangkara fell straight to the ground, and Sakya Pandita won the tenth parasol. It's said that Buddhism survived in Tibet because of that.

As an old saying has it, "Tibetans ruin it for themselves by having too many deities." They think they have to practice one, then they have to practice another, then a third, and a fourth. It goes on and on, and they end up not accomplishing anything; whereas, in India, a meditator would practice a single deity for his entire life, and he would reach supreme accomplishment. It would be good if we were to take this attitude. If we practice Vajrasattva, it is perfectly complete to simply practice that single yidam. We don't have to be constantly shifting to different deities, afraid we will miss something, because there is absolutely nothing missing in any single yidam we may practice.

A line from one tantra says, "I apologize for accepting and rejecting the yidam deity." Sometimes we feel tired with a particular practice, thinking, "It's enough, practicing this one yidam!" Then we give up that one and try practicing another one, then after a while, another. Try not to do this.

As I have said many times, if you accomplish one buddha, then you accomplish all buddhas. If you attain the realization of one yidam, automatically you attain realization of all yidams at the same time. Of course, there is nothing wrong with practicing more than one. The point is to not skip around between them.

Practice whichever yidam you like best. You will naturally feel more inclined toward one yidam than another, and this feeling is a very good indication of which yidam you are connected to. The basic guideline is to choose the one that inspires you the most. Then once you choose, practice it continuously.

There are no essential differences among the yidams. You cannot say there are good or bad yidams, in that all yidam forms are included within the five buddha families. No buddha family is better or worse than any of the others—not at all. People's individual feelings do make a difference, in that some people want to practice Padmasambhava as their yidam, while some want to practice Avalokiteshvara or Buddha Shakyamuni or Tara. The preference varies from person to person due to karmic inclination; however, there is no distinction in quality among yidams. If you take the one hundred peaceful and wrathful deities as your yidam, you have everyone included.

Once you reach accomplishment, you have simultaneously accomplished all enlightened qualities, regardless of which yidam you practice. It doesn't make any difference. For example, when the sun rises, its warmth and light are simultaneously present. If you accomplish one buddha form, you simultaneously accomplish all buddha forms. The reason is that all yidams are essentially the same; they differ only in form, not essence. The fundamental reason one attains accomplishment is because of recognizing mind essence while doing the yidam practice. The real practice is recognizing rigpa, and you use the yidam as the external form of the practice. Even though every yidam manifests various aspects of different qualities, in essence they are all the same.

People describe the rising sun in all sorts of different ways: Some say that when the sun rises, it's no longer cold; others say there's no more darkness, or it's become light and they can see. It's the same with describing the different aspects of the enlightened state, in which all the qualities, such as wisdom, compassion, and capability, are spontaneously present.

Try to see yidam practice as a gift that the buddhas have given to us because we have requested it. When we take refuge, we are asking for protection, to be safeguarded, and the real protection lies in the teachings on how to remove the obscurations and how to attain realization. The real protection is the yidam practice. Through it we can remove what needs to be removed and realize what needs to be realized, and thereby attain accomplishment.

Although we have this enlightened essence, it is like a butter lamp that is not yet lit, not enlightened yet. We need to connect with, to touch it with a lit butter lamp in order to light our own. Imagine two butter lamps together: One is not lit; the other is already enlightened. The one that is as yet unlit has to bow to the other in order to get the light.

In the same way, we already have the buddha nature, but we haven't caught on to it yet. We haven't recognized it, trained in it, and attained stability. There is great benefit in connecting with those other "lamps," because they have already recognized their buddha nature, trained in it, and obtained stability. Our butter lamp is ready to be kindled, to catch the flame, but it hasn't recognized itself, it hasn't trained, and it hasn't yet attained stability.

Yidam practice has great benefit. Mipham Rinpoche had a vision of Manjushri, his supreme deity, and through that he became a great pandita, an extremely learned scholar. Many of the Indian mahasiddhas practiced Tara sadhana. They combined recognizing mind essence with the yidam practice and attained accomplishment. All the life stories of those who became great masters tell of yidam practice. You never hear of anyone saying, "I achieved accomplishment and didn't use any deity. I didn't need to say any mantra." The yidam deity practice is like adding oil to the fire of practice; it blazes up even higher and hotter.

Vajrakilaya Practice

Introduction to Sangtik Phurba

Tsikey Chokling Rinpoche

From the teacher Samantabhadra, within the equality of the four times—the time beyond the past, present, and future—in the place of the dharmadhatu buddhafield of Akanishtha, unmoved from the infinite, uncreated, great buddha mind, the unobstructed miraculous manifestation of the mandala of the basic nature itself arose as the form of Dorje Shonnu and consort. From this union of nondual wisdom and means, the various wrathful ones in the ten directions and the mandala of the sons of Phurba openly emanated and were taught the hundred thousand excellent classes in the different tantras of the activity phurba.

The lineage thus starts with the great teacher Samantabhadra and passes to Vajrasattva, Vajrapani, and to Dakini Leykyi Wangmo, from whom the Brahmin Miyi Thopachen and others received it. Then, after the Phurba tantras appeared in the world of men, the pandita Prabhahasti was able to defeat the anti-Dharma non-Buddhists of Golden Island in India, converting them into faithful Buddhists. Acharya Garab Dorje received the actual Phurba tantra from Vajrasattva on the peak of Mount Malaya, as he states in his tantras. Acharya Hungchenkara and other awareness holders removed the accomplishment section[ii] as terma from the garden of Silwatsal Sitavana, Cool Grove.

After non-Buddhists had devastated the Sandalwood Grove by fire, Acharya Padma (Guru Rinpoche) restored it to its former state, by the power of his phurba. Vimalamitra, by brandishing his phurba, reversed the flow of the Ganges, split its upper and lower parts, and destroyed the man-eating sea monsters dwelling there. The Nepali Shri Manju at

Drakmar Gongchen smashed the rocky hills to pieces and subdued the rock goblins and thieves. Similarly, the Nepalese woman Kalasiddhi struck the rock of Kargong with her phurba, displaying marks of accomplishment.

The Lady of Kharchen, Yeshe Tsogyal, brandished her phurba at an attacking wolf and caused it to stumble and fall. Having tamed the ancestral goblins, she was renowned for taming a succession of spirits. Such was the extent of her liberating activity, that she could kill and revive ravens as well as resuscitate human corpses. These and many other examples show her innumerable marks of attainment. Tsogyal's disciple Menu Gyalwey Nyingpo, carrying a garland of ravens, could cause them to fall to the ground, with his mystic contemplation (of Phurba). Palgyi Lodro of the Lo clan, striking the army barracks with his phurba, utterly defeated the Nepalese army. Nyag Jnana completely destroyed his brothers' enemies. There are these and many other related tales.

The power of the Phurba practices destroys the outer enemies and obstacle makers and subdues the inner obscuring emotions, thus allowing practitioners to actualize the realization of dharmata, the inexpressible. Once the Phurba tantras reached Tibet, Phurba became the method for pacifying obstacles, demons, and hindrances. The *Phurba of Vitotama*, having been brought to Nepal, pacified all obstacles immediately. In the material sense, magical expressions are actually manifested; in the subjective sense, the inconceivable blessings of liberation in the dharmadhatu are attained. As Phurba is the lord of activity of all the buddhas, Phurba masters had long, prosperous lives and were renowned far and wide for their great powers.

The great tertön Dharma King Chokgyur Lingpa has three classes of Phurba: *gyū* or Mahayoga, the *Zabdun Phurba; lung* or Anuyoga, the *Lungchen Dorje Kopa Phurba;* and the *men-ngag* or Atiyoga, this *Sangtik Phurba*. Jamyang Khyentse Wangpo has the hearing lineage, called the *Phrin las Phur pai gNad tig*. Both Khyentse and Chokling, as explained above, actualized the inner and outer marks of attainment. Thus are the authorizations of both the profound Terma tradition and the Hearing lineage completed.

As for the *Sangtik Phurba* having the marks of the heruka, it contains all of a heruka's qualities and accoutrements. He is a sambhogakaya representation with the heart of great compassion, able to liberate sentient beings. As the quintessential Phurba, the *Sangtik Phurba* has been the yidam of all the Choklings. It is the Atiyoga Phurba, the Phurba of the oral instructions. The practice is very efficacious for getting rid of all obstacles, being concise and easy to do, and it contains great blessings.

Phurba

Sangtik Phurba Lineage Supplication

Künzang Gyurmey Tsewang Drakpa

Künzang dorsem palchen heruka
Dorje chödang khandro leywangmo
Prabhahasti dhanasamskrita
Solwa debso barchey uljom shok

Samantabhadra, Vajrasattva, Great Glorious Heruka,
Vajrasharma and Dakini Karmeshuari,
Prabhahasti and Dhanasamskrita,
I supplicate you; may all obstacles be defeated.

Garab dorje lopon hungkara
Dorje tötreng tsal dang bimala
Balbang kalasiddhi kharchenza
Solwa debso barchey uljom shok

Garab Dorje and Acharya Hungkara,
Vajra Tötreng Tsal and Vimalamitra,
Kalasiddhi of Nepal and Princess of Kharchen,
I supplicate you; may all obstacles be defeated.

Chögyal yabsey chogyur dechen ling
Tsawa yanglak gyülung mengakgi
Gyüpey lama rinpar jön namla
Solwa debso barchey uljom shok

Dharma king, father and son, and Chokgyur Dechen Lingpa,
All successive lineage gurus

Of the root and branches, and of the tantra, texts, and instructions,
I supplicate you; may all obstacles be defeated.

> Tünmong tünmin ngöndrö gyüjang shing
> Lamgyi ngöpo yongdzog nyamlang pey
> Döchey lüla yeshe kurmin tey
> Dudjom pawoi gopang ngöngyur shok

Through purifying my being by practicing the general and special preliminaries,
As well as the entire main part of the path,
May this physical body ripen into the wisdom body.
Thus, may I realize the state of Dudjom Pawo.

The Sadhana of the Single Form of Vajrakumara:

According to the Sangtik Nyingpo Cycle:

Chokgyur Lingpa

NAMO VAJRAKUMARAYA:

For this activity practice of the:
Great Glorious Vajrakumara, condensed to the essence,:
Visualize all the objects of refuge before you.:

Lama könchog sumnam dang:
Heruka dang khandro ma:
Kyabyül gyamtso khyenam la:
Jangchub bardu kyabsu chi:

Gurus and Three Jewels,:
Herukas and dakinis,:
In all of you, the ocean of objects of refuge,:
I take refuge until enlightenment.:

Semchen kün gyi dön gyi chir:
Dzogpey sangye tobdö la:
Bardu chöpey düdül chir:
Palchen gopang tobpar ja:

For the sake of all sentient beings,:
I intend to attain complete buddhahood.:
In order to tame the maras, who create obstacles,:
I will attain the level of the great Glorious One.:

Powerful Transformation

Dorje tröpey zhedang chö༔
Tsönchen ngönpo barwa ni༔
Namkhai kyil ney tigpa shar༔
Hung gi özer chogchur tro༔

Vajra-wrath cuts through aggression.༔
The great, blazing blue color༔
Manifests as a drop in the center of space.༔
By light rays of HUNG radiating in the ten directions,༔

Nangsi purbu zhingkham gyur༔
Tingnag e-yi longkyil du༔
Dragchen pe-nyi lhachen teng༔
Hung yig yongsu gyurpa ley༔

Appearance and existence are the realm of Kilaya.༔
Amidst the space of the dark blue E,༔
Upon the great rock, lotus, sun, and Mahadeva,༔
From the transformation of the letter HUNG,༔

Dorje tingnag hung gi tshan༔
Özer chogtu barwa ley༔
Ngang nyi dorje chö-ying ley༔
Barwey trowo mizay pa༔

A dark blue vajra appears, marked with HUNG.༔
By dazzling rays of light blazing forth༔
From the vajra state of dharmadhatu,༔
The overwhelming, blazing Wrathful One appears.༔

Tingnag zhalsum chagdrug pa༔
Yeykar yönmar ü-ting zhal༔
Dragpöi chengu chogchur dray༔
Zheldang jagdril chetsig zhing༔

He is dark blue, with three faces and six arms.༔
His right face is white, his left one is red, and his central one is blue.༔
His nine eyes fiercely glare in the ten directions.༔
With open mouth and rolling tongue, he bares his fangs,༔

Powerful Transformation

A ralli yi drachen drogˢ
Mara minma metar barˢ
Utra gyenkhyil traseb tuˢ
Dorje chepey tshanpa yiˢ

Roaring the great sound ARALLI.ˢ
His beard and eyebrows blaze like fire.ˢ
His hair streams upward, markedˢ
In the middle with a half-vajra,ˢ

Tewar lama mikyö paˢ
Yeypa dangpo tsegu dangˢ
Barpey tse-nga chogchur zirˢ
Yönpa dangpo mepung dangˢ

With Guru Akshobhya in its center.ˢ
His first right hand holds a nine-pronged vajra;ˢ
His middle one aims a five-pronged vajra in the ten directions.ˢ
His first left hand holds a mound of fire;ˢ

Barpey khatvang tsesum dzinˢ
Tamey rirab purbu drilˢ
Dorje rinchen shogpa dengˢ
Langchen zhingpag tödu sölˢ

The middle one holds a trident khatvanga.ˢ
His last hands roll the sumeru kilaya.ˢ
With vajra-jewel wings outspread,ˢ
He wears an elephant and human skin above,ˢ

Tag-gi pagpey shamtab dzeyˢ
Tötreng tsharsum doshel dangˢ
Tökam namkyi ugyan chingˢ
Rinpo cheyi tsetran dangˢ

And a tiger skin as a skirt.ˢ
Wearing the threefold head garland,ˢ
His head is adorned with five dry skulls,ˢ
Each with jeweled points.ˢ

Drülrig lnga-yi chünpo gyen:
Tragzhag talwa namkyi jug:
Rüpey gyendrug lasog pey:
Palgyi chaychu kula dzog:
Shabzhi rölpey tabkyi gying:

Ornamented with wreaths of five classes of snakes,:
He is smeared with blood, fat, and ashes:
And wears the six bone ornaments and so forth;:
Thus, the tenfold glorious attire is complete on his body.:
His four legs are poised in the dancing posture.:

Deyi pangdu jorwey yum:
Khorlo gyendeb tingnag bar:
Yeypey utpal yabgül khyü:
Yönpey tötrag yabla tob:

On his lap is the consort of union,:
The dark blue, blazing Diptachakra.:
Her right hand, with a blue lotus, embraces the lord,:
And her left proffers a skull cup of blood.:

Langtsho gyeypey gyurbag chen:
Chag-gya ngayi gyenchang shing:
Yönkum yabkyi keyla tril:
Yeykang dewa chenpor jor:

She is endowed with the expressions of a fully bloomed maiden.:
She wears the five mudra ornaments.:
Her left leg, bent, embraces the waist of the lord,:
And with her right leg extended, they are joined in great bliss.:

Chiwor om hung tram hrih ah:
Yeshe ngayi dagnyi chen:
Neysum om ah hung gi tshan:
Kusung tugsu jingyi lab:

At the top of his head are OM HUNG TRAM HRIH AH,:
Possessing the nature of the five wisdoms.:

Powerful Transformation

The three places, marked with OM AH HUNG,⸫
Are blessed as body, speech, and mind.⸫

Yabkyi sangney hung yig ley⸫
Dorjei tewar hung gi tshen⸫
Yumgyi khasang pam yig ley⸫
Pemar nyima ang gi tshen⸫

From the letter HUNG at the secret place of the lord,⸫
A vajra appears, marked with HUNG in the center.⸫
From the letter BAM in the secret space of the consort,⸫
A sun appears, marked with ANG in her lotus.⸫

Dewa chenpöi yingsu röl⸫
Bapu dorje chepa dang⸫
Natshog dorjei gotrab söl⸫
Purbui tsa-tsa kartar trug⸫

They sport in the space of great bliss.⸫
His body hairs are half-vajras,⸫
And he wears an armor of crossed-vajras.⸫
Kilaya tsa-tsas shoot out like stars.⸫

Tugkar ökyi gurkhyim ü⸫
Pema nyidey denteng du⸫
Yeshe sempa dorje sem⸫
Karsel dorje drilbu dzin⸫

In his heart center, amidst a dome of light,⸫
Upon a seat of lotus, sun, and moon,⸫
Is the wisdom being, Vajrasattva.⸫
White and luminous, holding a vajra and bell,⸫

Nyemma dritö dzindang tril⸫
Kyiltrung shugpey sog-gi gau⸫
Rinchen cha-gyey nyiday teng⸫
Dorje ngönpöi tewa la⸫

He embraces Atopa, who is holding a knife and skull.⸫
He is seated cross-legged, and within his life-sphere,⸫

Powerful Transformation

Upon a jewel octagon, sun, and moon,⁏
Is a blue vajra with a deep blue HUNG,⁏

Nyimey tengdu hung ting ga⁏
Takor drugu rangdrar chey⁏
Deley özer rabtrö pey⁏
Chog chüi gyalwa tamchey kyi⁏

Resting upon a sun in its center,⁏
Around which are the self-resounding nine syllables.⁏
Immense light rays stream from them,⁏
Making pleasing offerings to the body, speech, and mind⁏

Kusung tugla nyechö pül⁏
Kusung tugkyi jinlab nam⁏
Om kar ah mar hung ting ni⁏
Pagdu mepa chendrang te⁏

Of all the victorious ones of the ten directions.⁏
All the blessings of body, speech, and mind⁏
Are invited as white OM, red AH, and blue HUNG,⁏
In an immeasurable amount.⁏

Rang-gi neysum timpa yi⁏
Wangkur jinlab ngödrub tob⁏
Deshek lama nyepar jey⁏
Chedang chamdrel nyamchag kang⁏

As they dissolve into my three places,⁏
I obtain the empowerments, blessings, and siddhis.⁏
The sugatas and gurus are pleased;⁏
Breaches with dharma brothers and sisters are amended;⁏

Khandro chökyong khönpa jang⁏
Dregpa tamchey leyla tsü⁏
Dudang damsi talwar lag⁏
Drowey gosum gribpa jang⁏

Grudges of dakinis and dharmapalas are cleared;⁏
All the drekpas are brought to action;⁏

Powerful Transformation

Maras and samaya-breakers are reduced to dust;˥
And all the obscurations of beings' three gates are purified.˥

Nangwa tamchey lhayi ku˥
Dragpa tamchey ngagkyi dra˥
Drentog yeshe rölpar gyur˥

All sights are the form of deities,˥
All sounds are the sound of mantra,˥
And thoughts are visualized as the display of wisdom.˥

The essence of your mind should be regarded˥
As Vajrakumara himself.˥

OM BENZA KILI KILAYA SARVA BIGHANEN BAM HUNG PHAT˥

Thus recite. Offer torma in the session breaks.˥
Visualize the glorious torma˥
To be the deity and receive the empowerments.˥
Begin by offering the flower.˥

Lama palchen heruka˥
Dorje zhönnu yabyum gyi˥
Dagla jingyi labney kyang˥
Kusung tugkyi wangchog tsöl˥

Guru Glorious Heruka,˥
Vajrakumara, lord and consort,˥
Please bestow the blessings upon me˥
And grant the supreme empowerments of body, speech, and mind.˥

Thus supplicate and visualize yourself as the deity.˥

Tormey lhayi neysum ney˥
Özer karmar tingsum trö˥
Rang-gi neysum timpa yi˥
Gosum dribpa malü jang˥
Kusung tugkyi wangtob gyur˥

Powerful Transformation

From the three places of the deity, the torma,༔
Three rays of white, red, and blue light stream out.༔
As they dissolve into my three places,༔
All the obscurations of the three gates are purified,༔
And the empowerments of body, speech, and mind are obtained.༔

Hung༔
Tornö tingnag drusum barwey ying༔
Tormey ngowo palchen heruka༔
Chomden dorje zhönnu trowo gyal༔
Yumchog drölma khorlo gyendeb ma༔

HUNG༔
The torma vessel is the blazing space of the dark blue triangle.༔
The torma essence is the great Glorious Heruka,༔
Bhagavan Vajrakumara, king of the wrathful.༔
With supreme consort, Tara Diptachakra,༔

Düdül trochu yabyum tratab dang༔
Seychog gokyong sungmay tshognam kyi༔
Düdir tugdam nyenpöi gochey la༔
Siji kuyi wangchog lüla tsöl༔

Mara tamers, ten dancing wrathful ones and consorts,༔
Supreme sons and all gatekeepers and protectors,༔
Open the gate of your powerful samaya now,༔
And bestow upon my body the majestic, supreme body empowerment.༔

Lükyi neydön digdrib barchey söl༔
Jalü dorjei kuru drubpar dzö༔
Tsangyang sung-gi wangchog ngagla tsöl༔
Ngag-drib ngag-ngen digkug selwa dang༔

Clear away physical sickness, evil forces, misdeeds, and obscurations.༔
Make me accomplished in the rainbow body vajra form.༔

Powerful Transformation

Bestow upon my speech the supreme empowerment of
  Brahma's voice.
Clear away speech obscurations, stuttering, and muteness.

Drag-ngag tuyi ngödrub tsaldu söl
Trödrel tugkyi wangchog semla tsöl
Yidrib nyobog gyalney zhiwa dang
Dechen tugkyi ngödrub tsaldu söl

Please grant the siddhi of the power of wrathful mantras.
Bestow upon my mind the supreme mind empowerment of
  simplicity.
Pacify mental obscurations, insanity, strokes, and illness.
And grant the siddhi of the mind of great bliss.

Shen yang cheykha bötong dokpa dang
Dugching dangsems denpa tsharchö la
Tshesö paljor gyepar dzeydu söl

Moreover, avert sorcery and evil spells,
Annihilate viciousness and ill-will,
And increase life, merit, splendor, and wealth.

At the end of the mantra, attach:

KAYA VAKA CHITTA SARVA SIDDHI PHALA
ABHIKHENTSA HOH

Thus receive the empowerment.
For the torma offering, say:

Ram yam kham gi torma segtor trü
Tongpey ngangley lungmey tö-gye teng
Bhrum ley bhandza yangzhing gyachei nang
Go ku da ha na ley sha-nga dang

RAM YAM KHAM burns, scatters, and washes away the torma.
From the state of emptiness, upon wind, fire, and a skull-stand,
A vast and extensive skull cup manifests from BHRUM.
Inside it, the five meats appear from GO KU DA HA NA,

Powerful Transformation

Bi mu ma ra shu ley dütsi nga:
Khachö nyima dawa dorje tshen:
Meylung jorwey dütsi zhushing khöl:
Langwey khordey dangma chunam du:

And the five nectars flow from BI MU MA RA SHU.:
The lid is a sun and moon marked with a vajra.:
By the joining of fire and wind, the nectar melts and boils.:
The steam gathers all the essences of samsara and nirvana.:

Rig-nga yabyum kurgyur dechen jor:
Khachö cheypa jangchub semsu zhu:
Damtsig yeshe dütsir nyimey drey:
Döyön chötrin namkha gangwar gyur:
Om ah hung ho:

They become the forms of the five families of lords and
  consorts, united in great bliss.:
Together with the lid, they melt into bodhichitta.:
Samaya and wisdom mingle indivisibly as nectar.:
An offering cloud of desirable objects fills the sky.:
OM AH HUNG HOH:

Raising the right hand and pointing the left,:
Consecrate with the mudra of joined thumb and finger.:

Hung:
Chökyi yingkyi podrang ney:
Chomden dorje zhönnu dang:
Sungma damchen khordang chey:
Sipey purbu drubpa dang:

HUNG:
From the palace of dharmadhatu,:
Bhagavan Vajrakumara,:
With your retinue of protectors and pledge-holders,:
Please bestow the empowerments and siddhis,:

Powerful Transformation

Wangdang ngödrub tsölwey chir:
Yeshe trowo shegsu söl:
Yeshe trowo shegney kyang:
Takdang tsenma tenpa dang:
Kilaya yi ngödrub tsöl:
Benza sama dzah:

In order that I may accomplish the Kilaya of existence.:
Wrathful Wisdom, please come.:
Wrathful Wisdom, having now arrived,:
Manifest the signs and marks:
And bestow the accomplishment of Kilaya.:

VAJRA SAMA DZAH:

Hung:
Lamey chog-gi chöpa dampa ni:
Yeshe ngayi özer nampar tro:
Döpey yöntan ngayi rabgyen te:
Tugdam zhindu chider sheysu söl:

OM SHRI VAJRAKUMARA DHARMA PALA SAPARIVARA PUSHPE DHUPE ALOKE GANDHE NAIVIDYA SHAPDA PRATICCHAYE SVAHA:
MAHA PANTSA AMRITA KHARAM KHAHI, MAHA RAKTA KHARAM KHAHI:
OM BENZA KILI KILAYA SAPARIVARA IDAM BALING GRIHANANTU MAMA SARVA SIDDHIM ME PRAYATSA:
OM BENZA KILI KILAYA DHARMA PALA SAPARIVARA IDAM BALINGTA KHA KHA KHAHI KHAHI:

HUNG:
This sacred and supreme offering:
Radiates the light rays of the five wisdoms,:
Fully adorned with the five desirable objects.:
As your heart-samaya, accept these as you please.:

OM SHRI VAJRA KUMARA DHARMA PALA SAPARIVARA:
PUSHPE DHUPE ALOKE GANDHE NAIVIDYA SHABDA PRATICCHAYE SVAHA:
MAHA PANCHA AMRITA KHARAM KHAHI:

Powerful Transformation

MAHA RAKTA KHARAM KHAHI༔
OM VAJRA KILI KILAYA SAPARIVARA IDAM BALING GRIHANANTU༔
MAMA SARVA SIDDHI MEM PRAYACCHA༔
OM VAJRA KILI KILAYA DHARMA PALA SAPARIVARA༔
IDAM BALINGTA KHA KHA KHAHI KHAHI༔

Hung༔
Tabkyi chöpey drodön du༔
Jamdang nyingje gangdül wa༔
Sangye trinley dzogdzey pey༔
Purpa trinley lhala chagtsal tö༔

HUNG༔
Skillfully acting for the sake of beings,༔
Through love and compassion you tame whoever needs help༔
And perfect the activities of the buddhas.༔
To all Kilaya Activity deities, I prostrate and offer praise.༔

Hung༔
Machö trömey dezhin nyi-ying ley༔
Dechen lhündrub barwey kurzheng pa༔
Chomden palchen dorje zhönnu dang༔
Yumchog drölma khorlo gyendebma༔

HUNG༔
From the uncontrived space of suchness beyond constructs,༔
Manifests the blazing form of spontaneously present great bliss,༔
Bhagavan great Glorious Vajrakumara,༔
With the supreme consort, Tara Diptachakra.༔

Dorje purbu rigpa dzinnam dang༔
Trochu yabyum zaje söje tshog༔
Seychok nyerchig tromo goma zhi༔
Shona dagnyi sadag kyebüi tsog༔

All knowledge-holders of Vajrakilaya,༔
The ten wrathful ones, lords and consorts, hosts of devourers and slayers,༔

Twenty-one supreme sons, four female wrathful gatekeepers,ː
Hosts of shvanas, sovereigns, bhumipatis, and great beings,ː

Purbey sungma damchen gyamtsor cheyː
Mi-ngön yingney neydir kurzheng laː
Damdzey chinang sangwey chöpa dangː
Dütsi rakta tormai chöpa zheyː

Together with the ocean of Kilaya protectors and pledge-holders,ː
Manifest here in form, from invisible space.ː
Accept the samaya substances of outer, inner, and secret offeringsː
And the offerings of nectar, rakta, and torma.ː

Dagchag pönlob yönchö khorchey namː
Gosum longchö cheypa sungwa dangː
Kusung tugkyi ngödrub tsöl du sölː
Neydön barchey tamchey shiwa dangː

For all of us, master and disciples, patron and recipient, together with our retinues,ː
Protect our three gates as well as our riches;ː
Bestow the siddhis of body, speech, and mind;ː
Pacify all illnesses, negative forces, and obstacles;ː

Tsesö paljor tamchey gyeypa dangː
Khamsum sisum wangdu düpa dangː
Dra-geg talwar lagpey trinley dzöː
Chekha purkha tamchey dogtu sölː
Tashi delek jungwar dzeydu sölː

Increase our life spans, merit, glory, and riches;ː
Magnetize the three realms and the three existences;ː
Perform the activity of reducing animosity and obstructing forces to dust;ː
Turn away all black magic and evil spells;ː
And make auspicious goodness manifest.ː

*Thus, entreat.*ː

Powerful Transformation

Dissolve the wisdom beings into yourself.
Let the loka beings leave to their own places.
Through this, all obstacles will be pacified
And all wishes will be fulfilled.
Therefore, exert yourself in this.
This profound oral instruction
Is concealed for the sake of future times.
May it meet with the person of right karma.

SAMAYA GYA GYA

The incarnated tertön Chokgyur Dechen Lingpa revealed this from the Tsari-like Jewel Rock (Tsadra Rinchen Drak) and established it in writing at the upper retreat of Künzang Dechen Ösel Ling. Padma Gargyi Wangchuk (Jamgön Kongtrül Lodrö Thaye) then wrote it down. May virtuous goodness increase.

(Note: Now follows a short way of finishing the sadhana after the main mantra, according to the instructions of Tulku Urgyen Rinpoche.)

Hung
Nangsi purbu kyilkhor nam
Tugkyi tigle chenpor tim
Palchen poyi yingnyi ley
Kusung tugkyi kyilkhor sel

HUNG
Appearance and existence, the entire Kilaya mandala,
Dissolve into the great mind bindu.
From the space of the great Glorious One,
Manifests the mandala of body, speech, and mind.

Thus, perform the dissolution and emergence.

Gatsa gatsa sobhava nam
GACCHA GACCHA SVABHAVA NAM

Powerful Transformation

Thus, let the worldly guests take leave.

Hung
Miney yeshe kyilkhor du
Kusung tugsu lhündrub ney
Dorje zhönnü gopang tob
Drowa küngyi paldu shog

HUNG
Having attained the spontaneous accomplishment of body, speech, and mind
In the mandala of nondwelling wisdom,
May we attain the state of Vajrakumara
For the splendorous benefit of all beings.

Hung
Rigdzin tsalchang jinlab küngyi dag
Sipey purbu ngödrub küngyi ter
Mamo khandro nyurgyog trinley chen
Purpey kyilkhor lhayi trashi shog

HUNG
May the power-wielding vidyadharas, the lords of all blessings,
The existence Kilaya, the treasury of all accomplishments,
And the mother dakinis, endowed with swift activities
All be present as the auspicious mandala deities of Kilaya.

Thus, create virtuous goodness through dedication, aspiration, and the utterance of auspiciousness.

• • •

This was translated under the guidance of Tsikey Chokling Rinpoche, Gyurmey Dewey Dorje, and Orgyen Tobgyal Rinpoche by Erik Pema Kunsang.

A Roar to Delight Heruka

Clear Instructions on the Deity for the Single-Mudrā Vajrakumāra of the Secret Heart Essence Cycle

Karmey Khenpo Rinchen Dargye

NAMO VAJRAKUMĀRAYE

Your body of blissful wisdom with seven qualities
Is unsurpassed dharmadhātu, devoid of extremes.
As your compassion without reference embraces all beings,
I bow to you, liberator of the ten fields, Śrī Heruka!

Beginning with this homage and supplication to the head of the maṇḍala, inseparable from the great treasure revealer Vajradhāra, here I will briefly explain the unelaborated development and completion stage meditations for the single mudrā (i.e., solitary form) of Vajrakumāra, derived from the *Secret Heart Essence* cycle in a manner suitable for daily practice.

First of all, it is extremely important to apply your mind to the various phases of the preliminary practices, engendering such qualities as faith, compassion, and renunciation. Then visualize the objects of refuge present before you as being your Vajrayāna spiritual teacher indivisible from Vajrakumāra and surrounded by clouds of ḍākas and ḍākinīs. Alternatively, you can simply bring to mind the meaning of the words as you recite them, with a vivid and heartfelt recollection of the qualities of the objects of refuge. Assuming you are already well trained in the general preliminary practices from either the old (Nyingma) or new (Sarma) traditions, it is not necessary to meditate elaborately on the objects of refuge. In this context, you should regard Vajrakumāra as containing everything—viewing him as the indivisible ground and fruition of the Vajrayāna or the essence of the result (i.e., the unity of appearance and emptiness, which constitutes dharmakāya). *The Magical Key to the Storehouse*[1] states,

> In taking the mudrā's maṇḍala as the path,
> The resultant Vajrayāna
> Thus takes the result itself as the path.
> One's body, speech, and mind
> Are conjoined with vajra body, speech, and mind.
> Understanding this is taught to be the Vajrayāna.

This is ultimate, or essential, refuge and intention to achieve enlightenment (*bodhichitta*). As for the four or six types of external teachers, the way to rely on these spiritual friends—in whom firm faith and belief form the very root of the path—is explained in detail in the various sūtras and tantras and in their commentaries. In particular, you should refer to the life stories of the great meditation masters of India and Tibet. Reflect on these stories and apply their message to yourself.

Dharmakāya is that which is empty in essence and devoid of the duality of arising and ceasing. Its luminous nature is sambhogakāya. Nirmāṇakāya is compassion manifesting itself in manifold ways. The teacher who is the epitome of these three kāyas is the final, singular refuge—the recognition of the essential meaning of self-awareness.

Heruka literally means "blood drinker." Such a deity can be conceived of in three ways: externally, as an imputed deity, meaning the infinite maṇḍalas of the peaceful and wrathful gods and so on; internally, as one's body purified into a maṇḍala of the conquerors, in which the five poisons are the five wisdoms, the five aggregates are the five conquerors, and the five elements are the five consorts, and so forth; or secretly, as sound and appearance manifesting unobstructedly as the essence of the deity from the dynamic potential of self-aware emptiness.

---

[1] *Bang mdzod 'phrul sde*, according to the text, but likely *phrul lde*. This is a *snying-ma* tantra.

Similarly, ḍākinī has references on three levels: externally, as the ḍākinīs of the twenty-four lands formed through either primordial wisdom or karma; internally, as the ḍākinīs that are the channels, winds, and essences residing in the five wheels; or secretly, as the ḍākinī of great bliss—thus, the empty essence representing wisdom, which unites with the ḍāka of skillful means, or the unobstructed play of awareness.

The text expresses that there are many objects of refuge when it says, *the ocean of objects of refuge,* referring to all that exists. *Until enlightenment* means that—although it is not the case that refuge is no longer needed after enlightenment—the final refuge is one's own mind manifesting dharmakāya, at which point, the object of refuge and the subjective mind seeking refuge become inseparable and indistinct. This is similar to one who wants to enter the king's palace from the outside wall; one doesn't need to go in again after reaching the inside.

You should think, "As I presently do not have the ability to help all living beings, I wish to attain the state of a fully perfected buddha for this purpose." The demons obstructing this pursuit are the four māras. These consist of the demon of the lord of death, the demon of the aggregates, the demon of the afflictions, and the demon of the son of gods. In order to subdue these demons, the texts states, *I will attain the level of the great Glorious One.*

Regarding the meaning of this, all obstacles and demons are subsumed within phenomena and persons. Generally speaking, all phenomena can be subsumed within the eighteen elements, which are contained within the twelve faculties, and these faculties fall within the five aggregates. The self of the person is based on the self-conceit of thinking, "I am." The self of phenomena originates from regarding that which is subsumed within the five aggregates to be real or truly existent.

The "absence of self" refers to both its nonexistence with respect to the person, (i.e., the absence of self of the person) and its nonexistence with respect to the eyes, nose, and other phenomena, (i.e., the absence of self of phenomena.) Apprehending the two forms of self constitutes the ignorance binding one to cyclic existence. Based on the apprehension of a self in phenomena, the ignorance that apprehends a personal self then originates. From this, formations and everything else arise.[2] If this igno-

---

2 I.e., the other twelve links of dependent origination.

rance is reversed, both apprehender and apprehended become empty, as is explained in Nāgārjuna's *Praise of Basic Space* (*Dharmadhātustava*), which states,

> Seeing the meaning of the two types of absence of self
> Will terminate the seed of saṃsāra.

It is therefore important to understand that all demons are destroyed by the wisdom that realizes the absence of self.

The main practice begins with the three samādhis or meditative absorptions, which, as they are important yet difficult to understand, I will explain in some detail. The essence of the first of these three is the natural dharmakāya. Its name, the "samādhi of dharmakāya suchness," conveys a meditative state that rests by naturally falling into the unmistaken and uncontrived—an empty essence and a clear nature that are maintained without distraction in the resonance of empty luminosity devoid of thoughts and grasping. The word *vajra* connotes this in the text. As the *Joint Application* (*mnyam sbyor*) explains,

> The vajra is said to be emptiness.

And the *Mirror of Explanatory Tantra* (*bshad rgyud me long*) states,

> Having the nature beyond distinctions—
> This is explained to be the vajra.

What is meant by this nature devoid of distinctions? *The Fundamental Verses of the Middle Way* (*Mūlamadhyamakakārikā*) states the following,

> A nature must be uncontrived
> And not rely on anything else.
> A nature that changes into something else
> Would never make sense.

What is the purpose of this first meditative samādhi? All sentient beings have forever been confused by ignorantly apprehending a self and therefore roaming throughout cyclic existence. The remedy for this is meditating without grasping on the empty and luminous dharmakāya beyond elaborations. As this represents the meditation of the Secret Mantra, in which the result serves as the path, it is from this resonance of the dharmakāya that the other two form-bodies emerge.

Second is the "all-illuminating samādhi." It has the essence of deep compassion. The term refers to the appearance or light of deep compassion dawning for beings who have not understood emptiness. It serves the purpose of bridging, by means of compassion, the empty essence of suchness free of elaborations and the causal meditative absorption of the seed syllable, which involves characteristics. In other words, the illusory display of the seed syllable arises out of the resonance of emptiness that is imbued with a core of compassion. It is specified in the text with the words *Vajra-wrath cuts through aggression*. Here *wrath* actually refers to compassion in that deep compassion for the "ten fields of compassion" destroys anger in a wrathful manner. It is often referred to with the phrase "incredible methods that liberate the lower realms," meaning to embrace with deep compassion those whose evil actions are destined to lead to the lower realms.

Third is the "samādhi of the seed syllable," the essence of which is spontaneous awareness itself. The name refers to this absorption being the cause for the supportive palace and the supported deities. Its purpose is to serve as the cause for the generation of the maṇḍala's deities. It is specified in the text with the words *The great, blazing blue color manifests as a drop in the center of space*. This means that the dark blue syllable HUNG, symbolizing the unity of emptiness and deep compassion, appears as a large and unchanging drop. Meditate with firm confidence that your own awareness appears in the form of HUNG, which you visualize to be hanging like the moon in the expanse of the sky. HUNG is derived from *ha*, which belongs to the Sanskrit words *grāhaka*, meaning "apprehended," and *hagrahaca*,[3] meaning "apprehender." When the vowel *ū* is combined with the consonant *ś* the result is *śū*, which implies emptiness or zero and is called *lato*.[4] Therefore, HUNG is the seed or causal syllable of the emptiness of apprehender and apprehended. From it, light radiates in the ten directions—meaning up and down and in the other eight

---

3 *Apprehender* in Sanskrit is *grāhya*. The origin of *hagrahaca* is unknown.
4 I've been unable to understand *lato*. Presumably *śū* is referring to *śūnyatā*, "emptiness."

directions. With this you should simply regard the external and internal universe along with all of existence as being the paradise of Vajrakīlaya. Here it is not necessary to meditate on a more elaborate celestial palace.

Vividly bringing to mind the celestial palace in this way, visualize a triangular deep-blue E at its center. Meditate that this itself is a deep blue seat made of light and featuring a ridge that resembles a fence coming up to approximately knee-level. Otherwise, you can visualize a large and expansive deep-blue triangle with its thin tip facing downwards and large mouth upwards. One point faces forward or, alternatively, one point faces to the back, while there is a gate in the front.

In the middle of this rests a large vajra-rock of deep blue star sapphire that is triangular and made of light. At its center is a variegated lotus with a hundred thousand petals, in the middle of which is placed a sun disc. On top of the sun disc, visualize an overturned black Mahādeva and red Umādevī, lying on her back. Both are naked and without ornaments, hands joined in supplication. Alternatively, visualize Mahādeva to the right, lying overturned and with an angry expression. He has golden red hair, is draped in a tiger-skin robe, and holds a trident in his right hand and a skull cup filled with blood in his left. To the left is red Umādevī lying on her back with an expression of lust. She wears a leopard skin and holds a trident in her right hand and a skull cup with blood in her left.

On top of them, the letter HUNG transforms into a deep blue vajra with another HUNG marking its center. Light blazes forth from it, spreading outward and making offerings to the conquerors. It purifies the sins, obscurations, and suffering of all beings. As the light returns inward, the great brute of inexhaustible, burning wrath arises out of the wisdom primordially present in the basic space, the vajra-suchness. When the root text describes this, it is indicating that the deity is made attractive by "ugliness" and the other nine expressions of dance.[5]

As all of the expressions of wrath are complete within the inexhaustible wheel of adornments, the deity's body is dark blue to represent the unchanging nature of things. He has three faces in order to symbolize the three bodies (the center blue face being dharmakāya, his

---

[5] The nine expressions of dance are: the three expressions of the body—attractive, heroic, and ugly; the three expressions of speech—ferocious, laughing, and frightening; the three expressions of mind—compassionate, angry, and peaceful.

left red face sambhogakāya, and right white face nirmāṇakāya). His six hands symbolize the six perfections. Alternatively, you can understand the right white face to symbolize body, the left red face speech, and the middle dark-blue face mind. His violently furious nine eyes bulge and scorch the ten directions, representing the nine vehicles or the nine types of wisdom. His three craving mouths are wide open, showing his red tongue, which is curled-over yet fast-moving like lightning. He also shows his four clenched fangs, which are white like a snow mountain.

He utters ARALLI. The mantra VAJRA ARALLI can be construed to imply "without stains, the single vajra-stake flies," meaning "to bask unobstructedly in all activities," or "the vajra destroys enemies." I suspect the latter, translated by Zhalu Lotsawa, is perhaps more correct. His mustache, eyebrows, and beard are a golden red that blazes like fire. They are disheveled and fierce looking. Most of his golden red hair is twisted upward and tied in a bun, while the remainder stands on end.

Inside his hair is an *uṣṇīṣa* or head protuberance, the tip of which is a dark blue vajra made of light. At the center of this vajra is a jewel throne with eight elephants supporting it, two on each side. Imagine that on top of this rests a lotus, sun, and moon supporting Akṣobhya in his sambhogakāya form without consort. His right hand touches the ground and left hand rests in equipoise while holding a five-pointed vajra. Also at the tip of the *uṣṇīṣa* inside the hair of Vajrakīlaya's consort, visualize the dark blue Locanā, also in sambhogakāya form. Her right hand touches the ground and left hand rests in equipoise while holding a vajra that contains the elephant-supported throne, and so on, as described above.

As for the deity's six hands, his first right hand holds a nine-pointed vajra with spread prongs, which symbolizes having destroyed the concepts of the nine grounds. According to some followers of the old translations, the nine grounds of the three realms refer to the following: the ground of hell, where there is downfall; the ground of hungry ghosts and animals, which is submerged; the ground of humans, where merit can be accrued; the ground of the wind, which moves everything; the ground of gods, the upper realm; the ground of clouds, which shows signs; the ground that's fragrant with stainless wisdom; the ground of name, sign, and faculty.[6] Nevertheless, the more common explanation is

---

6 The text only enumerates eight. There appears to be one missing. Also some are vague in their meaning. Further study is required.

Powerful Transformation

to associate these with the ten bodhisattva grounds,[7] which is also said to be more correct.

The deity's middle right hand holds a five-pointed vajra, which he aims in all directions. It represents concepts of the five poisonous afflictions purified into the five types of wisdom. His upper left hand holds a blazing fireball, while his fingers display the threatening gesture that symbolizes burning away the darkness of ignorance. His middle left hand holds a three-pronged trident khaṭvāṅga, representing the purification of the three poisons. His lower hands twist a sumeru-kīla, or stake of the king of mountains. Be it permanence, nihilism, self, or characteristics—whatever object of grasping this stake penetrates, it will unfailingly unite it with the state of unchanging great bliss. The term *stake of existence* refers to the three realms of existence perfected into the deity's maṇḍala. Thus the sumeru-kīla is such that the stake's upper knot is associated with the formless realm; the handle, with sixteen wings, along with the lower knot are associated with the form realm; and the sea monster's desirous mouth and the stake's sharp tip are associated with the desire realm. These three realms of existence are also the maṇḍala of body, speech, and mind. This is all explained in the *Summarized Intention of the Single Heart-Stake Tantra* (*thugs kyi phur gcig rgyud kyi dgongs dril*), as follows,

> In order to liberate the six causes[8]
> Of the realm of existence with plants, trees, and so on,
> The deity's six hands hold up a nine-pointed vajra to cut the obscurations to omniscience,
> Throw a five-pointed vajra that destroys the five poisons,
> Hold a khaṭvāṅga that liberates the three poisons,
> Make a threatening gesture that destroys concepts,
> And twist a stake that liberates evil.

You should understand the visualization in this way.

---

7 *sa bcu phyin chad kyi rtog pa* literally means "the concepts after the ten grounds." Perhaps the text should read *tshun chad*, which would mean "up to the ten(th) ground." It is likely referring to the nine "concepts" associated with the nine grounds of the path of meditation, described in the *Abhisamayālaṅkāra*.

8 Probably referring to six types of causes found in Abhidharma texts.

The deity's right arms are of the nature of Akṣobhya and left arms Ratnasaṃbhava. Similarly, his right and left wings are also of the nature of Akṣobhya and Ratnasaṃbhava, respectively. This is why the text states, *With vajra-jewel wings outspread.*[9] You can also imagine that his right vajra-wing is embedded with vajras, and his left razor-wing is embedded with jewels.

The deity wears the fresh hide of an elephant on his upper body, because he has tamed the elephant vehicle of Indra. Having liberated Brahmā, he also wears a skin of the so-called great field. As a lower robe, he wears a tiger skin, due to having subdued the one-eyed tiger-faced daughter[10] of Mahāgraha Surya, the sun god. He wears three long necklaces of wet, dry, and old skulls to symbolize his having liberated the three rudras. In some Vajrakīlaya traditions, such as that of Rok, the deity is said to have a crown of dry skulls, a long necklace of wet skulls, and bracelets/anklets of bone fragments. Our particular treasure text, however, follows only the former explanation.

The deity's head ornaments consist of a crown of five dry skulls that are connected by means of intestines strung through the skulls' openings. Although they appear as skulls from the outside, inside they have small rooms with the five blood-drinkers without consorts. Their right hands display their given mudrā with its appropriate implement and left hands hold skull cups filled with blood. They also wear the glorious charnel ground adornments, as they are usually described. Alternatively, it is also acceptable to visualize them without ornaments. Vajra Heruka resides in the center skull of the deity's center head. On the right head, Buddha Heruka is positioned in the center skull, while Padma Heruka takes this position on the deity's left head. In the dry skulls on the head of Vajrakīlaya's consort, the mothers of the five blood-drinkers sit with Vajrakrodhī at the center.

The peaceful forms of five buddhas are situated inside jewels that act as top-ornaments for the skulls, with Akṣobhya in the main position of the center face, Vairocana on the right, and Amitābha on the left.

---

9 Because Akṣobhya and Ratnasaṃbhava are from the vajra family and jewel family, respectively.

10 I haven't been able to determine to whom this is referring. Some suggestions have included Uttar Phalgunī, one of the Nakṣatra deities. Tiger-faced one (f) in Sanskrit is Vyāghrāsya; however, how this connects to Surya is less clear.

As above, you can visualize their ornaments and garments in whatever way is most comfortable. Visualize Locanā and the other four consorts situated in the top-ornaments of the skulls located on the head of Vajrakīlaya's consort. I have explained the visualization[11] of the five families of peaceful and wrathful deities in connection with the deity's dry skull ornaments, but the actual visualization takes place later on when inviting the empowerment deities. When practicing in a simplified manner, it is sufficient to only recall that the five dry skulls have the nature of the five buddha families.

Because he has subdued the vicious *nāgarājas* (serpent kings), Vajrakīlaya is adorned with bunches of serpents belonging to the five different castes. According to the Māyā tradition of the *Transmitted Precepts*, these refer to: white serpents of the warrior caste as a head ornament; yellow serpents of the merchant caste as earrings; red serpents of the Brahmin caste as a neck ornament; black untouchables [serpents] as a short necklace; and green serpents of the laborer caste as anklets, bracelets, a middle-length necklace, belt, and so on. Another option, as explained in the *Difficult Points of the Peaceful and Wrathful Deities* (*zhi khro'i dka' gnad*), is similar to the above, except that variegated red Brahmin serpents act as a hair band, green serpents of the laborer caste act as anklets, and black untouchables [serpents] are the deity's belt. You can use either of these explanations.

The eight charnel ground adornments are worn by the deity who procured them as victory loot, having subdued the great and terrifying lord of the charnel ground, Rudra. *He is smeared with blood, fat, and ashes* means that, having taken Rudra's wife under his control and played with her in the manner of having no attachment, he has three drops of blood on his two cheeks and the tip of his nose. He has three smears of fat on his goatee, as a result of having taken the twenty-eight Īśvarīs under his control. Also having subdued his own sister, Shimukhale, he has a blot of great ash on his forehead in the shape of a triangle.

The six bone ornaments are associated with the six perfections. The circular bone ornament on his head has a thirty-two piece web, from within which the deity's hair stands up. There is also a latticework of

---

11 The text reads *bsgom bya'i sa khong gi zhi khro*. I cannot make sense out of *sa khong*.

bone hanging from his crown of dry skulls. His two ears have two bone earrings. His neck has a sixteen piece webbed bone ornament. Brahmā's thread—also called ash/dirt—refers to a thread worn by non-Buddhist priests on top of dried dung, which serves as a reminder and pledge to Brahmā. In order to subdue such individuals, the heruka wears this thread as a crossed garland, hanging from both shoulders on his upper body. It is made from corpse hair and bones and rests on an outline made from great ash. Alternatively, the sixth ornament can be a four-spoked bone wheel on his front and back.[12] In the context of the path, these six ornaments symbolize the five poisons, along with stinginess, being purified into the six perfections. Specifically, the bone wheel is the perfection of wisdom; the earrings, discipline; the neck ornament, patience; the belt, diligence; Brahmā's thread, concentration; and the bracelets and anklets, generosity. In the context of the fruition of the path, they represent the six families.

The glorious charnel ground adornments described here have a number of different enumerations. *The Practice Framework of the Eight Transmitted Precepts (bka' brgyad sgrub khog)* states the following,

> Possessing the five wisdoms, the deity wears a crown of skulls;
> Understanding the meaning of the supreme vehicle, a wet elephant hide;
> Not abandoning saṃsāra, a shawl of human skin;
> Destroying the two forms of aggression, bunches of black snakes;
> Spontaneously accomplishing the four activities, a tiger skirt;
> Extracting the nectar of saṃsāra, smears of fat;
> Controlling passion, drops of blood;
> Severing birth and death, blots of great ash;
> Spontaneously accomplishing the three bodies, three garlands;
> Being invincible, the vajra-armor;
> And burning the forest of ignorance, the fireball of wisdom.

---

12 The text reads, *mdun rgyab gnyis su mdo non rus pa'i 'khor lo*. I cannot ascertain the meaning of *mdo non*.

The vajra-armor and fireball are added to the basic eight charnel ground ornaments, making the ten glorious adornments. Alternatively, the illuminating adornment of fire and the dominating adornment of wings can be added to the basic list of eight. The great treasure revealer Chokgyur Lingpa has stated that this explanation comes from the *Tantra of Viśuddha* (*yang dag gi rgyud*).

The scholar-practitioner Tsele Rinpoche offers a similar explanation. He describes the eight charnel ground ornaments, eight glorious adornments, and two illuminating ornaments based on the Māyā tradition as follows,

> The skin of the great field is the ornament of bodhichitta;
> The wet elephant hide is the ornament of supreme, great strength;
> The tiger skirt is the ornament of consuming the ferocious;
> The bunches of black snakes are the soft and smooth twisted ornaments;
> The three garlands of skulls are the ornaments of approaching the three kāyas;
> The drops of blood are the ornaments of being attached with compassion;
> The blots of great ash are the ornaments of enlightened activity that subdues;
> The smears of fat are the ornaments of the nectar of the ultimate.

The eight glorious adornments, replete from time without beginning on the body of the great Glorious One, are as follows,

> Hair standing up straight is the adornment of turning back saṃsāra;
> The vajra garuḍa wings are the adornment of wisdom and means;
> The blue-red crown is the adornment of dominating saṃsāra and nirvāṇa;
> The crown vajra is the adornment of enhanced awareness;

Powerful hide-armor is the adornment of moving with
    brilliance;
Nondual joining is the adornment of the wisdom consort;
A hero's iron is the adornment of averting harm and evil;
Burning up afflictions is the adornment of vajra-fire.

The commentary of *Yungtön Dorje Palwa* states,[13]

The majestic adornments of sea monsters blaze with splendor;
The adornment of the sun and moon is the unity of wisdom
    and means;
The adornment of wisdom fire averts ferocious beings;
The adornment of sickle fangs severs birth and death;
The adornment of vajra-wings pervasively fulfills the needs of
    others;
The adornment of the vajra-coat wields authority;
The adornment of powerful hide-armor traverses others to the
    ground of enlightenment;
The adornment of the iron cross averts harm and evil.

The two "illuminating ornaments" are the sun and moon above the left and right ear. Alternatively, *Lhajerog* explains them to be garlands of the sun and moon.

The ten glorious adornments mentioned in the *Root Tantra of the Condensation of Bliss—The Manifestation of Wrath* (*bde 'dus rtsa rgyud khro bo mngon byung gi rgyud*) are also similar in language. In our tradition, the supreme awareness-holder Chokgyur Lingpa's treasure teaching *Dispeller of Obstacles: Accomplishing the Guru's Heart* (*thugs sgrub bar chad kun sel*) explains the eight charnel ground adornments and the glorious adornments as follows. The root text states,

The three garments worn are the three poisons purified;
The three applied ointments are unmoving arising and
    cessation;

---

13 This seems to be an alternative enumeration for the eight glorious adornments.

The two fastened ornaments are the indivisibility of saṃsāra and nirvāṇa, and so forth—
The deity is thus complete with the terrifying, violent adornments of the charnel ground.

Regarding the glorious adornments, the text states,

The secure and unrivaled throne;
The blazing fireball of unfathomable wisdom;
The snake ornaments untouched by the fetters of afflictions;
The three wings of unimpeded service to others;
The silk ribbons fulfilling the wishes of disciples;
The six bone ornaments completing the six perfections;
The jewel garland with which thoughts become the ornament of basic space;
The garuḍa ornamenting the deity's head, taming all ferocity;
The nine forms of dance that invite frolicking—these are said to be the ten glorious adornments.[14]

You should visualize in this way. Otherwise, the explanation explicit in the root text of the *Secret Essence* is that the vajra-wings and six bone ornaments are added to the eight charnel ground adornments to arrive at ten (glorious adornments). Alternatively, you can understand that when the practice text says *the six bone ornaments*, and so forth, this refers to the glorious adornments—specifically, the water lily and sun/moon ornaments above the ears.

Covering the deity's genitals are either five-colored or green silk streamers that have three stakes (*kīla*) hanging from them. Three streamers hang from each hip. The heads of sea monsters adorn the deity's shoulders and lower body. This adornment symbolizes that the deity's deep compassion embraces all beings and will never forsake them, just as a sea monster clutches its catch and will not release it.

The deity's four legs are in the dancing posture, with the right legs raised and the left legs extended. This symbolizes defeating the army

---

14 Here again the text only seems to enumerate nine.

of the four demons and leading sentient beings with the four means of attraction.

The deity's consort Diptachakra, the appearing aspect of wisdom, is joined with him, resting in his lap. She is a great, blazing dark blue that represents dharmakāya's singular essence. Her two hands symbolize wisdom and means. Her right hand holds a water lily, as she embraces the father's neck. Her left hand offers a skull filled with nectar to the father's mouth. The texts describe her as *a fully bloomed maiden*, meaning that she is like a sixteen-year-old in the prime of youth, proportionally plump and resembling freshly polished gold. She sports the five mudrās, which [are similar to the six bone ornaments but] exclude the Brahmā thread.[15] Her left leg is raised and twisted around the father's waist, while her extended right leg joins the father in the great bliss of basic space. Her two legs symbolize dominating the two truths of saṃsāra and nirvāṇa.

As the root treasure text only explicitly mentions the five mudrās, it is sufficient to visualize only this much for an unelaborated style of practice. For a more detailed version, however, the great omniscient siddha[16] has explained that the details of the consort's appearance are the same as the father's, apart from a leopard-skin skirt taking the place of the tiger skin.

Invite the empowerment deities—the five buddhas and their retinues—so they fill the sky and empower you with a stream of wisdom-nectar. This nectar fills your body and purifies stains. The liquid overflows upward and transforms into a crown of the five buddhas, as previously described. For a less elaborate version, you can also visualize the hand-implements of the five buddhas giving the empowerments. Most unelaborated, you can also merely visualize the buddhas' root syllables of OṂ HŪNG TRĀM HRĪḤ ĀḤ on your head. Regardless of the amount of detail you use, bring to mind that they are of the nature of the five wisdoms.

Symbolizing that the three places of the body are enlightened body, speech, and mind, visualize Vairocana at the father's head, Amitābha at his throat, and Akṣobhya at his heart center. On the mother's body, vi-

---

15 This point was clarified by Khenpo Namdrol's *lha'i dkyil 'khor thim byang* on page 28.
16 This may be referring to Chokgyur Lingpa.

sualize Dhātīśvarī at her head, Pāṇḍaravāsinī at her throat, and Locanā at her heart. In a simplified way, you can imagine that both the father and mother's three places are marked by the letters OṂ ĀḤ HUNG. These three letters grant the blessings of the bodily marks of enlightenment, the sixty-four branches of the "voice of Brahmā," and nondual wisdom, respectively.

The syllable HUNG at the father's secret place transforms into a five-point blue vajra with a HUNG marking its center. The head of the HUNG faces the mother. The BAṂ at the mother's secret space transforms into a red lotus with four petals, at the center of which is a red ANG syllable atop a sun that represents the condensation of siddhis. It is connected to the drop-channel (*bindu-nāḍi*). *They sport in the space of great bliss*,[8] as the text states, and instantaneously complete all the paths and grounds.

The deity's billions of body hairs are all half-vajras, and he wears armors of variegated vajras. This refers to the vajra-coat (i.e., armor with a variegated vajra design), the hide-armor of power, and the iron vajra-cross mentioned in the context of the ten glorious adornments. The variegated vajra-armor is worn on the upper body, the red hide-armor of power at the waist, and the black iron cross is worn on the lower body. In actuality, these three pieces are to be associated with purity. In no way are they actually iron, hide, and so on; rather, they are made from the self-appearance of wisdom. When the text refers to sparks of *Kīlaya tsa-tsas shoot out like stars*,[8] it means that these stakes burst forth like stars and stream continuously outward in infinite number, just like the flying sparks from burning iron that is hit with a hammer.

At the deity's heart center, inside a dark blue tent-like enclosure of light, rests the wisdom being, Vajrasattva, atop a seat comprised of a lotus, sun, and moon. His body color is clear white, and he holds a vajra and bell while sitting in the vajra-posture. In his lap, he embraces and joins with Vajraṭopa, who—sitting in the crossed-legged position of religious observance (*vrata/brtul zhugs*)—holds a hook-knife and skull in her right and left hands, respectively.

At Vajrasattva's heart center is a radiant dark blue eight-part or octagonal jewel. In the tradition of the Kīlaya tantras, this jewel is said to be flat. According to the oral transmission tradition of Vajrakilaya (*phur pa'i lung lugs*), it is said to be eight-sided, brown, and shaped like a tent. In any case, a red sun rests on top of the eight-part jewel that's acting as a throne. On top of that is a white moon, and on top of that is a nine-point vajra (which is a five-point vajra in the tradition of the oral transmission). At its center is a sun, on top of which is a dark blue syllable HUNG. It is encircled by the syllables OṂ VAJRA KĪLĪ KĪLAYA HUNG PHAṬ, which are green with a red tinge.

The syllables begin in front of the HUNG, face inward, and are arranged clockwise. During the approach phase of recitation, the syllables are unmoving, like stars encircling the moon. During the close approach phase, the syllables move in a circle that resembles a firebrand. During the phase of accomplishment, the syllables emit and receive light, like the messenger of a king. During the phase of great accomplishment, when performing specific activities, or when receiving siddhis, the syllables should resemble a broken beehive. This and other information can be found in Tendzin Jangchub Nyima's *Notes on Approach and Accomplishment* (*bsnyen sgrub kyi zin bris*), based on instruction from the masters, or in the *Mirror of Great Clarity: A Listing of All Approach and Accomplishment Instructions* (*bsnyen sgrub chig dril zin tho rab gsal 'phrul gyi me long*). For daily practice, you should visualize the circling of the syllables, emission of light, and so on, in a manner that combines all the different forms of approach and accomplishment into one.

With respect to the heart recitation described in relation to approach and accomplishment, you should refer to the two instruction books.[17] In the context of the speech recitation, there are three types of so-called blocked recitations, in terms of shape, sound, and meaning. For the first, you should only visualize and focus one-pointedly on the shape of the syllables. For the second, focus only on the sound of the syllables. For the third, focus one-pointedly on the meaning of the mantra, which is explained in the *Latter Tantra of Renunciation* (*nges par 'byung ba phyi ma'i rgyud*). OṂ represents the five wisdoms. VAJRA means vajra-wisdom. KĪLĪ KĪLAYA implies a naturally pure stake. SARVA indicates all. BIGHANEN means obstacles. BAM means to suppress. HUNG means to condense. PHAṬ means to burn beyond existence.

---

[17] It appears these are no longer available. The "heart recitation" presumably refers to the meditation associated with the third of the "recitations of body, speech, and mind" found in other Kīlaya texts.

For daily practice, the recitation-visualization that is explicitly described in the practice text for the emanation and collection of light is as follows: As the Kīlaya mantra garland spins, it emanates its own sound. It also emits white light rays that make pleasing offerings to all the conquerors. The blessings of body are collected in the form of a white OM and dissolve back into the deity's forehead; imagine that you receive the siddhis of enlightened body. Similarly, red light rays emit outward and make pleasing offerings of speech. The blessings of speech are collected in the form of a red AH and dissolve into the throat; imagine that you receive the siddhis of enlightened speech. Dark blue light rays emit outward and make pleasing offerings of mind. All the blessing of mind are gather by a dark-blue HUNG syllable and dissolve into the heart; imagine that you receive the siddhis of enlightened mind.

When practicing in an elaborate fashion, visualize that innumerable offering goddesses emerge from the light rays. For the pleasing offerings of the body, they offer the five sense objects to all the conquerors. The pleasing offerings of speech are amrita, rakta, and bali. The pleasing offerings of the mind are joining and liberation.

Then Vairocana, Akṣobhya, and Amitābha—the vajra-essence of conquerors' body, speech, and mind—are invited and dissolve into your three places. Also visualize that various types of light rays radiate outward to make offerings to the noble beings and please the bliss-gone-ones, teachers, and bodhisattvas. These light rays also mend broken samaya with spiritual brothers and sisters. They pacify the *grudges of ḍākinīs and dharmapālas* and encourage them to enact their activities. They command the arrogant demons, such as the group of thirty arrogant demons, and place them under oath to protect the Buddhist teachings. They reduce to dust the demons and *damsi* that obstruct the attainment of enlightenment. Finally, the light rays cleanse the obscurations and habitual tendencies of the three doors for the six classes of beings and lead them to the state of becoming Vajrakumāra.

All appearances are the form of Vajrakumāra; all sounds are the sound of Kīlaya; all thoughts are the play of wisdom. In brief, your three doors are inseparable from the three secrets of Vajrakumāra. Meditate that all of existence is the maṇḍala of the body, speech, and mind of Vajrakumāra.

Regarding the practice of unifying the approach and accomplishment with the recitation mantra, the *Root Tantra of the Peaceful and Wrath-*

ful Deities from the Eight Transmitted Precepts (bka' brgyad zhi khro rtsa rgyud) states the following,

> Beginning by placing OM and PHAT,
> And beautifying in the middle with twelve. . . .

From the *Latter Tantra of the Mantra of the Eight Transmitted Precepts* (bka' brgyad phyi ma sngags kyi rgyud),

> With the pride of being Vajrakumāra,
> If you constantly recite the vajra-recitation with your mind,[18]
> You will obtain the blessing and siddhis of the mantra
> And undoubtedly obtain
> The power of the buddhas to liberate false guides.

The recitation mantra has a fourfold establishment. Taking the syllable HUNG as an example, it is comprised of HA, U, and M. The essence of HUNG, primordially abiding as basic space and wisdom, is established by the essence of things (*dharmatā*). The form of HUNG, appearing as a syllable, is established by the nature of the subject (*dharma*). It is also established through its capacity to accomplish the vajra-mind, and through the blessings of being the vajra-mind seed syllable of the teacher Vajradhara. Based on this fourfold establishment, the recitation of HUNG is the direct cause for accomplishing the vajra-mind. This is the function of the mantra.

• • •

I have received many times this brief explanation, emphasizing the visualization instructions for the development stage daily practice of Vajrakilaya's Secret Heart Essence, *in both elaborate and abbreviated forms, directly from the mouth of the great treasure revealer, Chokgyur Lingpa, who is inseparable from the second Buddha, the Lotus-Born One, Padmasambhava. I wrote two short lists to remember the important points, when he was explaining the daily practice to the monastic assembly, which marked the beginning of my interest. I later had the*

---

18 *rdor blzas rig pa rtag blzas na* should perhaps read *rig pas*.

opportunity to ask many questions regarding the specifics of how to meditate on this practice. Thinking that I would forget these points, due to my meager intellect, I considered writing down the instructions. But it's said that writing such texts only serves to usurp the teaching of those who are truly accomplished scholar-practitioners. Also, under the pretense of being busy serving my teachers, when in fact I was distracted with my own mundane interests in food and clothing, this project got left behind. Later, after many requests from the monastery's lamas, Tokden Phakchok also repeatedly mentioned that it would be helpful if I were to formalize this text. In particular, Ngawang Lhundrub—a practitioner of the profound two stages of mantra—made an emphatic request that I was unable to deny. Therefore, I, Khenpo Pema Drime Lodrö, (Karmey Khenpo Rinchen Dargye)—a lazy, wandering man of mere technical skills whose head has touched the feet of the great treasure revealer and king of dharma, Chokgyur Lingpa—started writing this at Yelphug Namkha Dzong Gyurme Ling and finished it in a hut in south-east Yermo Che at the maṇḍala of speech, Ogmin Karma Temple. May all obtain stability in habitually regarding appearances as divinely pure and thus destroy the beginningless habituation to fixating on the impure. In the end, may we enter the city of Srī Heruka.

Sarva Mangalam
Virtue!

• • •

This manuscript was found in Nubri's Rö monastery. It had many mistakes and I was worried that the recension of the text would become completely lost. Therefore I, Trülku of Chokgyur Lingpa Pema Gyurmey, edited the words and text; if I have contravened the words of the holy masters, I confess and apologize.

This translation represents my best attempt at both accuracy and understandability for a reader possessing a basic familiarity with Vajrayāna. It was completed with the sincere wish that practitioners of the Chokling Tersar's Vajrakīlaya of the Secret Heart Essence *may have access to more detailed instructions. This does not represent a complete "critical translation" in any way. I have not consulted multiple versions of the manuscript; and I have relied largely on my own judgment in places where the text is unclear or appears corrupted. Nevertheless, I retain confidence that my efforts here are largely unmistaken. Whether it be due to a consideration of readership or simply a matter of the Tibetan erudite style, many references, names, lists, and quotations are not clearly explained in the original* text. Only through further consultation with learned teachers or detailed reference materials can all of these be clarified. This may leave some readers feeling discontent or even overwhelmed; however, I personally believe that it is not necessary to be overly concerned about these missing details for the casual use of this text to prove meaningful in enhancing one's practice. In places where ambiguities in the manuscript have been unresolvable, or where references have been easily explainable, I have made some sparing notes. My special thanks go to Khenpo Gyaltsan for answering a number of questions along the way, and also to Ani Laura Dainty, who thoroughly edited the first draft and made many meaningful recommendations. The translation was completed on March 5th, 2015, marking the festival celebrating the miraculous displays of the Buddha in Penang, Malaysia.

Ryan Conlon / Lungrik Rabsel

Clarifying Notes for the Sadhana of Vajrakilaya[iii]

Kyabje Dilgo Khyentse Rinpoche

As it is said, while trying to reach buddhahood, "The deeper our Dharma is, the stronger the obstacles of mara." If we are able to subdue these obstacles through the compassion of the Three Jewels, the ultimate antidote, they will not affect us.

The practice of Vajrakilaya is especially powerful in doing away with such obstacles. When Guru Padmasambhava was meditating on Yangdak Heruka in Asura Cave at Yangleshö in Nepal, the maras raised many obstacles. Guru Rinpoche then asked that the texts of the *Phurba Vitotama* tantras be brought from India. As soon as the texts reached Nepal, all difficulties subsided. In truth, Vajrakumara is the most powerful of all deities to dispel obstacles on the path toward enlightenment. This is why many great practitioners focus on the Vajrakumara practice to overcome adverse circumstances.

When actually engaging in this practice of Vajrakiliya, after the preliminaries, we get to the main part of the sadhana. This has instructions related to the form of the deity, dealing with visualization, followed by teachings on the deity's speech, focusing on mantra recitation. Finally, teachings related to the mind of the deity address the ultimate nature of the deity's wisdom heart. These three aspects manifest themselves to suit the needs of the beings to be benefitted, but they are not essentially different. The body aspect of the deity is inseparably united with the speech and mind aspects; likewise, the speech aspect is one with the body and mind aspects. A single pore of the Buddha's body, for instance, can perform the same enlightened activity as the Buddha himself. This is because the whole body of the Buddha is permeated with wisdom.

The form of the deity is not a body like ours, made of flesh and blood. If we could recognize the true nature of phenomena, we would realize that the whole universe and the beings in it are none other than the mandala of the Buddha's body. Although this is primordially so, beings are unaware of this nature and cling to the impure, deluded perceptions that are the causes of samsara. They apprehend the outer universe and the beings in a most ordinary, erroneous way.

To reverse this ordinary perception, we visualize phenomena as the display of wisdom deities. For this, we lay the foundation through the three samadhis and then meditate on the mandala itself and the deities it supports.

If we use these three samadhis, a sadhana ceases to be a mere development stage practice; it unites both development and completion stages. This is of vital importance: Without these three samadhis and the "four nails of concentration," development stage practice allows no accomplishment beyond ordinary, worldly siddhis. Supreme siddhis can be obtained only through uniting development and completion stages inseparably. This is why all the sadhanas of the Nyingma tradition begin with the three samadhis and include the practice of the four nails and other methods. Here we have:

> Vajra-wrath cuts through aggression.
> The great, blazing blue weapon
> Manifests as a drop in the center of space.
> By light rays of HUNG radiating in the ten directions,
> Appearance and existence are the realm of Kilaya.

This is a verse from Vajrakilaya's root tantra. Like a diamond, which cannot be cut by any other material, the vajra has seven extraordinary qualities: It cannot be cut or destroyed, it is hard, compact, and so forth. This signifies that the view, meditation, and action of the secret Vajrayana can cut through all deluded, dualistic thoughts, without being affected by them. Ordinary wrath is a mental poison, but vajra-wrath, though it manifests outwardly as wrath, is the expression of unwavering, infinite compassion. Through meditating on the vajra-wrath samadhi, one can annihilate the hatred present in the three realms of samsara. As it is said, "There is no sin greater than hatred, no greater asceticism than patience." Among the three mental poisons and the eighty-four thousand obscuring emotions, there is none that has more power to sever the life force of liberation than hatred. Nothing but emptiness can annihilate hatred and its seeds; therefore, the samadhi of vajra-wrath is emptiness manifesting as a wrathful deity. Emptiness is devoid of any concrete phenomena, characteristic, or condition, and therefore there is no room for hatred in emptiness. In other words, emptiness is primordially pure of hatred.

The great, blazing blue weapon

The wisdom mind of the buddhas is naturally permeated by all-encompassing compassion, the essence of emptiness. Like a sharp weapon, this great compassion has the power to sever all the obscuring emotions and sufferings of sentient beings. Blue symbolizes unchangingness and refers to the universal, objectless compassion of the buddhas, which can cut through all suffering without exception, throughout samsara and nirvana.

A natural compassion arises when we think about all those beings who have not realized this universally supreme emptiness that annihilates anger. This is what we should have in mind when meditating on the second samadhi, called the "samadhi of great compassion," or "all-illuminating samadhi."

Manifests as a drop in the center of space.

Thus, the first samadhi of the absolute nature, the "samadhi of suchness," is the realization of the emptiness of the universe and its contents, samsara and nirvana. The second is the expression of the essence of emptiness: compassion toward all beings who do not realize this emptiness. The indivisible union of emptiness and compassion permeates the whole of samsara and nirvana, just as space pervades the whole phenomenal world.

Within this vast expanse, as a drop appearing out of empty space, manifests a blazing dark blue letter HUNG, which symbolizes the nondual wisdom of all the buddhas and of Vajrakumara in particular. This syllable is like the seed of the mandala and of the deities in it; hence, the third samadhi is the "seed samadhi."

These three samadhis purify the three main sufferings of samsara: The samadhi of suchness purifies the deluded tendencies related to death; the samadhi of the great weapon of compassion, the all-illuminating samadhi, purifies the deluded tendencies related to the transitional state between death and the next birth (the bardo); and the samadhi of the seed syllable purifies the deluded tendencies related to rebirth.

The first samadhi is related to dharmakaya, the second samadhi to sambhogakaya, and the third to nirmanakaya. Thus these three samadhis lead to attaining the essence of the fruit, the three kayas.

The essence of the path is to strive toward buddhahood through uniting the means of great compassion and the wisdom of emptiness. The samadhi of suchness represents the wisdom of emptiness, the all-illuminating samadhi represents the means of great compassion, and the union of means and wisdom, which must never be separated, is the samadhi of the seed syllable.

Each of these three samadhis has the power to purify, to perfect, and to mature. As larger commentaries explain, these three—purification, perfection, and maturation—can be explained separately for each samadhi. But according to this higher form of development stage, it is permissible not to do so. Here, one develops the visualization within the simplicity of awareness, thus holding the vital force of the development stage. It is therefore not a fault if one does not know how to correlate these three transformations to each step of the development stage.

> By light rays of HUNG radiating in the ten directions,⁸
> Appearance and existence are the realm of Kilaya.⁸

We now come to the visualization of the mandala and the deities in it, which come about as the fruit or result of the three samadhis. The blue letter HUNG in the middle of space radiates light in all directions to all the universes, which, by nature, are pure buddhafields.

According to the relative causal vehicle, the "truth of the origination of suffering," is the cause, and the "truth of suffering" is the result. According to the secret Mantrayana, the "truth of the origination of suffering," the obscuring emotions, arise as the display of the kayas and pure lands of the buddhas. The "truth of the path" is the purification of our deluded clinging to phenomena, the ordinary perception we have of the universe and the beings in it. To purify this erroneous perception, we transform our ordinary perceptions, following the radiation of light from the letter HUNG, by visualizing the universe as the buddhafield of Vajrakilaya, with its eight cemeteries surrounding the wrathful palace. In this environment, the beings are all the display of the three kayas of the buddhas, abiding within the sphere of the "three aspects of liberation" (the ground of the empty nature; the path, which is beyond characteristics; and the fruit, which is beyond expectations.)

Amidst the space of the dark blue E,

First, meditate on the expanse of space, in the form of a vast blue inverted pyramid, wide open at the top, and within it, an ocean of blood.

Upon the great rock, lotus, sun, and Mahadeva,

Upon a vajra rock is the seat of all the wrathful deities, made of all kinds of precious substances. Upon it is an unsullied lotus symbolizing the means of compassion, and upon that is a sun disc symbolizing the awareness of emptiness. Upon these are Mahadeva and Umadevi, the former lying down facing the ground and the latter facing upward.

The three vajra stages follow: the stage of the seed syllable, the stage of its transformation into a symbol of the wisdom mind, and the stage of the transformation of this symbol into the full manifestation of the deity, as indicated here,

From the transformation of the letter HUNG,
A dark blue vajra appears, marked with HUNG.

The blue letter HUNG transforms itself into a dark blue vajra, whose prongs, five pointing up and five down, are not closed upon the central axis, but wide open, to indicate its wrathful nature. As the letter HUNG in its central knob radiates boundless light, the vajra changes into Vajrakumara.

Powerful Transformation

By dazzling rays of light blazing forth⸝
From the vajra state of dharmadhatu,⸝
The overwhelming, blazing Wrathful One appears.⸝

Although Vajrakumara appears in an exceedingly wrathful form, displaying the nine modes of wrathful dance, his wisdom mind never leaves the absolute expanse. When ordinary people get angry, their whole countenance changes, they become red and utter insults, telling others, "you are a thief, a rascal," while their mind is ablaze with anger. That is ordinary anger. Here there is no trace of ordinary anger; Vajrakumara abides in the nature of dharmakaya and never moves from the absolute expanse.

Although peaceful manifestations of the buddhas, such as Buddha Shakyamuni, have appeared and taught the Dharma, which, when practiced, can establish one on the path of liberation, there are beings who think that the Dharma is useless and meaningless. To benefit those beings and annihilate their inverted views, the buddhas manifest in wrathful forms. To free the consciousness of these antagonists in the absolute expanse is a feat, which only someone who has attained buddhahood can perform. This is why Vajrakumara appears in huge masses of fire, so formidable that none of the maras and rudras dare even to look at him.

He is dark blue, with three faces and six arms.⸝

His dark blue color symbolizes the unchanging dharmakaya. His three faces indicate that he completely possesses the enlightened qualities of the three kayas of the buddhas. He has six arms, symbolizing his having brought the six paramitas to perfection. His white right face, laughing loudly with a youthful expression, represents the nirmanakaya. His red left face, fiercely blazing with wrath, indicates the sambhogakaya, and his formidable blue central face symbolizes the dharmakaya. The nine eyes of these three faces represent the nine wisdom expanses, which are the purified aspects of the nine levels of the three realms of samsara. These nine eyes scan the ten directions in search of the maras to be annihilated. From his nose emanate countless HUNG syllables. His open mouth symbolizes that his activity for the benefit of beings is continuous throughout the three times and the fourth time, which is beyond time. His tongue rolls and vibrates like flashes of lightning. He displays his thirty-two teeth, especially his four fangs, which cut through the four kinds of birth.

Roaring the great sound ARALLI.§

The great sound ARALLI is Vajrakumara's mighty call to the dakinis. At the sound of this call, the dakas and dakinis, and the entire retinue of the wrathful ones, have no choice but to come and gather around Vajrakumara.

His beard and eyebrows blaze like fire.§

His beard and eyebrows emit sparks and flames, which burn down all maras and obstacle makers. Each of his hairs is shaped like the triangular blade of a kila, and his twenty-one thousand hairs stream upward like flames. One of the upper locks is knotted and bears a blue, five-pronged half-vajra, in the central knob of which dwells Akshobhya, the lord of the Vajra family.

His first right hand holds a nine-pronged vajra;§

His first right hand wields a nine-pronged vajra, symbol of his mastery of the meaning of the nine vehicles. His middle hand aims a five-pronged vajra in all directions, representing his ultimate realization of the five wisdoms. His first left hand holds a mass of fire, which destroys the five obscuring emotions. The middle one holds a trident khatvanga, symbol of Vajrakumara's endowment with the enlightened qualities of the three kayas and his power to cut through the three poisons (attachment, anger, and stupidity). The two lower hands roll a kilaya as huge as Mount Sumeru, which indicates Vajrakumara is performing all the buddhas' activity. Symbolic of the union of wisdom and means and his domination over the three worlds, his outspread wings point upward to the sky—the right one made of jewels and the left one of vajras.

Ornamented with wreaths of five classes of snakes,§
He is smeared with blood, fat, and ashes§
And wears the six bone ornaments and so forth.§

Thus, the tenfold glorious attire is complete on his body.§
His four legs are poised in the dancing posture.§

Vajrakumara is bedecked with the ten glorious ornaments. Three are garments: an elephant hide, a flayed human skin as upper garment, and a tiger's skin, with the head on Vajrakumara's right side, as a skirt. Three are garlands: one of dried skulls, one of decomposing heads, and one of fresh heads, symbols of his vanquishing the outer, inner, and secret attachment to the reality of phenomena.

Each of Vajrakumara's faces is crowned with a diadem of five dry skulls, symbolizing the purification of five poisons into five wisdoms. Garlands of small jewels hang from the diadem. On the top of these skulls are jewel-supports studded with the buddhas of the five families. Akshobhya is in the center, with Vairochana to his right, and then Ratnasambhava on his right side. Amitabha is toward the back, and Amoghasiddhi is on the left side.

He wears five wreaths of hissing snakes, symbolizing the destruction of anger: a wreath of white snakes, of the royal caste, as crown; a wreath of yellow snakes, of the merchant caste, as earrings; a wreath of red snakes, of the Brahmin caste, as his necklace; a wreath of blue snakes, of the commoner caste, as his long chest garland, and a wreath of black snakes, of the untouchable caste, as bangles for his arms and feet.

A triple line of cemetery ashes, symbol of the dharmakaya, marks his forehead. Representing the sambhogakaya, his cheeks are smeared with the heart-blood of Rudra, whose consciousness he has delivered. His throat is smeared with human fat, indicating the nirmanakaya. He also wears the six bone ornaments: crown ornament, garlands hanging from the diadem of skulls, earrings, necklaces, and arm and foot bangles, which symbolize the full attainment of the six paramitas. He wears blues scarves of silk and dons vajra-armor. Thus, as the spoils of his victory over Rudra, he has donned and made glorious the ten ornaments, which were Rudra's.

His four legs, which symbolize the "four legs of miracle," are poised in the dancing posture, the two right ones slightly bent, and the two left ones on the ground.

On his lap is the consort of union,§

Powerful Transformation

As a sign of the union of wisdom and means, he is in union with Diptachakra, the wrathful manifestation of Arya Tara, of a slightly lighter color than Vajrakumara. She has one head and two hands. She puts her right hand, which holds an utpala blue-lotus, symbol of purity, around Vajrakumara's neck. With her left hand, she offers him a skull cup filled with blood, symbol of the slaying of the obscuring emotions. She has the beautiful body of a youthful maiden, with a thin waist and fully bloomed breasts. She wears five bone ornaments, the same ones as Vajrakumara except the lattice of bones on the chest—and a leopard skin. They are united in great bliss. Although they appear formidable, their minds never part from the peace of the absolute expanse.

At the top of his head are OM HUNG TRAM HRIH AH.

Just as we visualize mantras when receiving empowerment, here, we visualize on the heads of Vajrakumara and his consort the syllables OM on the top of the head, HUNG on the forehead, TRAM at the right side of the head, HRIH on the nape, and AH on the left side of the head. These five symbolize the buddhas' mastering of the five pristine wisdoms through purifying the five poisonous emotions. On the three centers are the three syllables, representing the indivisible three kayas of all the buddhas: the white letter OM at the forehead, the red letter AH at the throat, and the blue letter HUNG at the heart. These indicate that the body, speech, and mind of all the buddhas are complete in the single form of Vajrakumara.

> From the letter HUNG at the secret place of the lord,
> A vajra appears, marked with HUNG in the center.
> From the letter BAM in the secret space of the consort,
> A sun appears, marked with ANG in her lotus.
> They sport in the space of great bliss.

The two secret organs of Vajrakumara and Diptachakra are not ordinary: the male organ is a five-pronged vajra, marked with the syllable HUNG, and the female one is a four-petaled lotus marked with the syllable BAM. They are united in inconceivable bliss.

> His body hairs are half-vajras,

As a symbol of his perfect buddha activity, he dons an armor made of intermingled, multicolored crossed-vajras, each of which has a white eastern prong, a yellow southern prong, a red western prong, a green northern prong, and a blue center prong. Coming out from all the pores of his skin, small incandescent kilas fill the space with sparks flying like shooting stars.

This concludes the explanation about the visualization of the physical manifestation of the deity. Second, for the mantra recitation:

> In his heart center, amidst a dome of light,⁑
> Upon a seat of lotus, sun, and moon,⁑
> Is the wisdom being, Vajrasattva.⁑
> White and luminous, holding a vajra and bell,⁑
> He embraces Atopa, who is holding a knife and skull.⁑
> He is seated cross-legged and within his life-sphere,⁑

Vajrakumara is neither concrete, like a clay, stone, or copper image, nor an inert emptiness, like a rainbow in space; he is permeated with the life of the heart-wisdom. To symbolize this, in his heart, within a dome of light, seating upon a white eight-petaled lotus, a sun, and a moon disc, is Vajrasattva, Adamantine Being, the size of a thumb's first joint. He is the wisdom deity, the peaceful form of Vajrakumara. Brilliant white, he holds a golden vajra at his heart with his right hand, and with his left hand lays a silver bell upon his thigh. He embraces his consort Atopa, in indivisible union. She is white, too, and holds a curved knife and skull cup. Vajrasattva sits in the vajra-posture, and his consort in the padma-posture.

> Upon the jewel octagon, sun and moon,⁑
> Is a blue vajra with a deep blue HUNG⁑
> Resting upon a sun in its center,⁑
> Around which are the self-resounding nine syllables.⁑

At the very center of Vajrasattva's heart is an eight faceted jewel, like a brown agate. Inside this jewel, upon a sun and a moon disc (each has the diameter of a pea), stands a blue vajra (the size of a grain of barley), in the central knob of which, on a sun disc, is a blue letter HUNG (the size of a mustard seed), surrounded by the nine continuously sounding syllables OM VAJRA KILI KILAYA HUNG PHAT. These extremely fine syllables, as though drawn with the tip of a hair, are seen in profile, with the left side of the syllable toward the center of the circle. The whole mantra garland circles the central syllable in such a way that one can read it as it revolves.

> Immense light rays stream from them,⸸
> Making pleasing offerings to the body, speech, and mind⸸
> Of all the victorious ones of the ten directions.⸸
> All the blessings of body, speech and mind⸸
> Are invited as white OM, red AH, and blue HUNG,⸸
> In an immeasurable amount.⸸

From the central syllable and the nine that surround it, rays of light emanate and make offerings to the buddhas and bodhisattvas, who dwell in the infinite buddhafields of the ten directions of space. These light rays please the buddhas in the continuum of their great bliss beyond samsaric stains.

> As they dissolve into my three places,⸸
> I obtain the empowerments, blessings, and siddhis.⸸

In return, the buddhas rain a shower of blessings in the form of innumerable syllables: white OM as the blessing of their bodies, red AH as the blessing of their speech, and blue HUNG as the blessing of their minds. When these syllables dissolve respectively into our forehead, throat, and heart, we receive the empowerments of the buddhas' wisdom body, speech, and mind, and become inseparably united with them.

> The sugatas and gurus are pleased;⸸

This offering of light pleases the victorious buddhas and bodhisattvas; when reaching our dharma brothers and sisters, it repairs any breach of samaya that may have occurred; when reaching the dakinis and protectors, it appeases their displeasure at our wrong conduct and practice; when reaching the evil forces that strive to harm the supreme doctrine, it reduces them to dust; when reaching beings of the six realms of samsara, it purifies their obscurations and dispels their sufferings.

In essence, we should then perceive all forms as the form of Vajrakumara, all sounds—including the barking of dogs, the neighing of horses, the chirping of birds, the howl of the wind, and the murmur of streams—as the sound of having amended breaches with dharma brothers and sisters: OM VAJRA KILI KILAYA HUNG PHAT. Thus, perceive all phenomena as the play of the absolute nature.

> The essence of your mind should be regarded
> As Vajrakumara himself.

Resting within the unmodified nature of mind, the primordial simplicity, understand that past thoughts are no more manifest, that future thoughts are yet to arise, and that present thoughts, when examined, have no substance. Perceiving all forms, sounds, and thoughts as the play of Vajrakumara's body, speech, and mind is called the "nail of unchanging wisdom," which remains unaffected by any kind of obstacle.

OM VAJRA KILI KILAYA SARVA BIGHANEN BAM HUNG PHAT

OM, the opening syllable, symbolizes the five wisdoms.
VAJRA, the adamantine vajra, refers to Vajrakumara and Diptachakra. It indicates that the vajra body, speech, and mind of Vajrakumara are unaffected by obstructing forces.
KI represents the ten herukas.
LI refers to the ten female wrathful ones.
KI indicates the secondary emanations, the devourers.
LA refers to the other secondary emanations, the slayers.
YA symbolizes the twenty-one supreme sons.
SARVA, all, refers to the further emanations, the Kilaya guardians.
BIGHA indicates the shvanas and others.
NEN represents the four rematis and others.
BAM refers to the bhumipatis and great beings.

HUNG invokes the wrathful ones and the glorious wisdom mind.
PHAT symbolizes the liberation of the consciousness of all the maras and obstacle makers into the absolute nature.

While reciting, you should combine the "activity nail of emitting and gathering light" and the "nail of unchanging wisdom."

Thus recite. Offer torma in the session breaks.⁞
Visualize the glorious torma⁞,
To be the deity and receive the empowerments.⁞

Reflecting on the vast benefit of this practice, which pacifies all obstacles, we must be determined to practice it.

• • •

Chokgyur Dechen Lingpa extracted this spiritual treasure from its place of concealment and offered it to Jamgön Kongtrül Rinpoche. This terma is considered to be shared by Chokgyur Lingpa and Jamgön Kongtrül Rinpoches. The practitioners of Tsadra Rinchen Drak always recite it at the beginning of their evening dharmapala prayers.

The Practice of the Single Form of Vajrakilaya

According to the Teaching of Sangtik Nyingpo

Orgyen Tobgyal Rinpoche

Sangtik Nyingpo is actually the destined terma belonging to Jamgön Kongtrül; however, Chokgyur Lingpa helped him out. Chokgyur Lingpa revealed the *Trilogy of the Secret Heart Essence* and then handed it over to him. Jamgön Kongtrül, himself, revealed what is called the *Three Yidams,* the three cycles of the guru of *Sangtik* and the three cycles of the dakini of *Sangtik.*

According to the dharma tradition of Chokgyur Lingpa, before enjoining any dharma protector to carry out the activities, one needs to visualize oneself in the form of the yidam deity.

There are three aspects to explaining Vajrakilaya, Dorje Phurba: how to visualize the deity's form, the body aspect; how to recite the mantra, the speech aspect; and how to rest in the samadhi of thatness, the mind aspect. In a separate text included here, Karmey Khenpo explains these in great detail from the Chokling Tersar. Karmey Khenpo says he wrote this text according to the personal instructions and advice of Chokgyur Lingpa, as well as from his own experience of teaching it several times to the congregation of monks, who practice it daily in his own monastery.

Chokgyur Lingpa had three types of Phurba termas: The Mahayoga one for tantra is the *Zabdun Phurba,* from the *Sevenfold Profundity;* the Anuyoga one for statements is the *Lungluk Phurba;* and the Atiyoga one for instructions *(men-ngag)* is this one, the *Sangtik, The Secret Essence Phurba.*

The men-ngag style means you simply visualize Dorje Phurba as a single figure, yourself as the yidam deity. The surrounding deities are the ten wrathful ones with their consorts, another ten with their consorts, and the gatekeepers. All of these together as one are called the men-ngag style. Otherwise, generally speaking, altogether there are seventy-five deities in the Phurba mandala.

The Nyingma tradition has two sections: tantra and sadhana. This belongs to the sadhana section, among which are the *Drupa Ka Gye*, or *Eight Heruka* sadhanas: *Manjushri Body, Lotus Speech, Vishuddha Mind, Amrita, Qualities,* and *Kilaya Activity*. This belongs to the *Kilaya Activity* sadhana.

For the most part, the siddhas of both India and Tibet attained complete accomplishment by means of Kilaya practice. The exposition connected to the empowerment for this practice explains this. The peaceful forms are Vajrasattva, Vajrapani, and Vajravidarana. The wrathful forms are Vajrapani (also); another form of the Vajrabhira, according to the new schools; and Vajrakilaya. These different deities actually have the same identity. They just look different, but their essence is the same.

When Padmasambhava was practicing Yangdak Heruka in the Asura Cave at Yangleshö and was about to attain the supreme siddhi of Mahamudra, the maras created many obstacles. To dispel these, he unfolded the mandala of Vajrakilaya and attained supreme accomplishment. Later, he bound all the spirits under oath in Tibet, also by means of Vajrakilaya.

The great pandita Vimalamitra was also an accomplished master of Kilaya practice. At one point, when there was a major obstacle, he raised and pointed his phurba, reversing the flow of the Ganges River. Later, when Padmasambhava opened the mandala and gave the transmission, instructions, and so forth to his close disciples in Tibet, Yeshe Tsogyal received that specific transmission, and with Vajrakilaya as her main yidam, she attained the accomplishments. At one point, by simply pointing her phurba, she made a crow fall to the ground.

Jamyang Khyentse Wangpo personally performed about fifty-five different types of Kilaya practice. His disciple Shechen Gyaltsab Pema Namgyal was also a master of Kilaya practice. And his disciple the omniscient Tashi Paljor, Dilgo Khyentse Rinpoche, also received the Kilaya practice from the Chöwang tradition, which he used as his extraordinary personal yidam. He also performed the full recitation according

Powerful Transformation

to seven different Kilaya traditions, including *Zabdun Phurba, Nyanglu Phurba,* and *Nyen-gyu Phurbu.*

These have been a few remarks on generating certainty by means of explaining the historical background, which is a requisite topic when giving teachings in the Kilaya tradition.

The many authoritative scriptures include original tantras like the *Bum Nag, The Black One Hundred Thousand,* and the *Bumtig.* Sakya Pandita also made expositions on Kilaya transmission, and Jamgön Kongtrül's vast commentary on it is included in *Gyude Kundu, The Collection of Sadhana Practices,* and so forth. So the Kilaya scriptures form a vast array.

In the Nyingma tradition itself, nearly every single tertön has revealed at least one Phurba terma, and some have revealed many. Among contemporary tertöns, Dudjom Rinpoche has two phurba practices, *Namchak Putrii* and the *Rekpong,* and Dilgo Khyentse Rinpoche has one called the *Nyakluk Phurba,* which is extremely detailed. But here we are studying the *Sangtik Phurba* of Chokgyur Lingpa.

What we have here is called the *Practice of the Single Form of Vajrakumara (Tib. Dorje Shonnu),* according to the teachings of *Sangtik Nyingpo.* Vajrakumara is just one of many in the vast teaching cycle of the Sangtik Nyingpo. There could be many ways to practice each, such as extensive or condensed; but this is the single form, called the single mudra.

Next comes the homage:

Namo Vajrakumaraya:

The first few lines are:

For this activity practice of the
Great Glorious Vajrakumara, condensed to the essence,:

Thus, this practice is a concise form of the great Glorious Vajrakumara. Here, I am not going to go through the practice word-by-word, because that would take several days, and Karmey Khenpo has already written an excellent, detailed explanation, which you are welcome to read and study. Also, it is not appropriate to just explain some of the words and leave others out. For instance, a lot could be said about just the term the great Glorious Vajrakumara *(palchen Dorje Shonnu)*, but I am not going to do that.

Visualize all the objects of refuge before you.⁂

In the sky before you, visualize the objects of refuge, including Vajrakumara, all the gurus, yidams, dakinis, and all the dharma protectors of this lineage. Imagine them as vividly present in the sky before you. In front of them, you take refuge, together with all other sentient beings as infinite in number as the sky is vast. With a respectful gesture, join palms in front of your heart; with a respectful voice, chant the lines of refuge; and with a respectful mind, entrust yourself to the meaning of taking refuge. As a daily practice, you would chant these four lines of refuge three times, but if you are doing it at the beginning of enjoining the protectors, then you only chant them once.

> Gurus and Three Jewels,⁂
> Herukas and dakinis,⁂
> In all of you, the ocean of objects of refuge,⁂
> I take refuge until enlightenment.⁂

The next four lines are for the bodhichitta resolve:

> For the sake of all sentient beings,⁂
> I intend to attain complete buddhahood.⁂
> In order to tame the maras, who create obstacles,⁂
> I will attain the level of the great Glorious One.⁂

The Drukpa Kagyü monasteries that chant the *Sangtik Phurba* have a particular style in which they chant refuge and bodhichitta three times each and then accompany the verses for the main visualization with a drum beat. In our tradition at Tsikey and Neten gompas, we simply chant the whole thing straight through from the beginning, without any repetitions or drums. However, since refuge and bodhichitta are indispensable at the beginning of any sadhana, they are repeated again and again.

Now the main part begins:

Vajra-wrath cuts through aggression.˸
The great, blazing blue color˸
Manifests as a drop in the center of space.˸
By light rays of HUNG radiating in the ten directions,˸
Appearance and existence are the realm of Kilaya.˸

Amidst the space of the dark blue E,˸
Upon the great rock, lotus, sun, and Mahadeva,˸
From the transformation of the letter HUNG,˸
A dark blue vajra appears, marked with HUNG.˸

By dazzling rays of light blazing forth˸
From the vajra state of dharmadhatu,˸
The overwhelming, blazing Wrathful One appears.˸

Among the three samadhis, the first sentence, *Vajra-wrath cuts through aggression,*˸ pertains to the samadhi of suchness. It refers to emptiness, but in a wrathful way. So what can cut through aggression, really? There is nothing other than compassion. So you could say that compassion is the real weapon against anger.

The great, blazing blue color[19] represents the second samadhi. It is the unity of emptiness and compassion, manifest *as a drop in the center of space,* which is the seed-syllable HUNG, the third samadhi. Karmey Khenpo provides a very complex commentary on this; but in short, that is the meaning.

Here, *vajra* refers to emptiness, because emptiness is endowed with the seven vajra qualities: uncuttable, indestructible, firm, solid, true, undefeatable, and unimpeded by anything whatsoever. Emptiness is, therefore, said to be like a vajra. The only weapon that can subjugate and destroy aggression or hatred is compassion. So that is the meaning of the great, blazing blue color.˸ This compassion that cuts through anger is inseparable from emptiness and manifests as a drop in the center of space˸

---

19 *Color* has an alternate translation, which means "weapon" as denoted by Kyabje Dilgo Khyentse Rinpoche's commentary. Orgyen Tobgyal Rinpoche is using this meaning here.

with the syllable HUNG. In this way, the three samadhis of suchness, illumination, and the seed syllable are complete.

The first two sentences actually appear with the same wording in most Kilaya practices, including the Kilaya from the oral tradition in the Sakya lineage. They can even be found in Sakya Pandita's Tibetan translation of the Indian Kilaya tantra. Jamgön Kongtrül's explanation of these two sentences is easier to understand, but I have used Karmey Khenpo's, since he was a personal disciple of Chokgyur Lingpa.

The HUNG appears in the middle of space just like a rainbow, a sun, or a moon in the center of the sky, and it radiates light in the ten directions. This light transforms whatever it touches into the buddhafield of Vajrakilaya. Vajrakilaya's buddhafield is a bit different in that it has a wrathful palace, a charnel ground, and wrathful ornaments and decorations. This means that all appearances, whatever is perceived, are the forms of Vajrakilaya; all sounds are the natural sounding of the Vajrakilaya mantra; and every state of mind is the all-pervasive, awakened state of Vajrakilaya. Even though the sadhana does not refer to the palace, Karmey Khenpo makes special mention of it. In the center of the palace is a dark blue Tibetan letter E, which refers to a triangular shape, like a platform.

What does the wrathful palace look like? Its walls are made of fresh, old, and new skeleton heads. It has water monster ornaments and human skin banners. Its crown ornament at the top of the palace is Rudra's heart, and so forth. Every wrathful deity is standing on a huge boulder, like a stone mountain.

Vajrakilaya is standing *upon the great rock, lotus, sun, and Mahadeva,*[8] which is actually comprised of two figures, one male lying face down and one female lying face up.

According to the explanations of the wrathful mandala, HUNG doesn't just float down and land in the center of the palace; rather, it strikes like a flash of lightning. Instead of immediately transforming into the deity, it first assumes the form of a dark blue vajra marked with the letter HUNG, which shines in all directions with dazzling rays of light that make offerings of all types to all the buddhas. The rays gather back the blessings of body, speech, and mind—and especially those of activities—which dissolve into the vajra. The vajra then transforms into Vajrakilaya.

Powerful Transformation

> He is dark blue, with three faces and six arms.
> His right face is white, his left one is red, and his central one is blue.
> His nine eyes fiercely glare in the ten directions.
> With open mouth and rolling tongue, he bares his fangs,
> Roaring the great sound ARALLI.
> His beard and eyebrows blaze like fire.

It is said that one face is awe-inspiring, another is laughing, and the other is roaring. Each face has three eyes, altogether nine that glare in the ten directions. His mouth is gaping and his tongue is rolled back, baring his fangs. In some of the Kilaya texts, it is said that one of the faces is clenching its teeth, but here all the mouths are open. You can see the rolled-up tongue and all four fangs. There are many explanations of the symbolism. For example, the three faces illustrate the transformation of the three poisonous emotions, and the twelve fangs represent the reversal of the twelve links of independent origination. The tongue that is rolled back roars with the sound of ARALLI, or joyful laughter. His moustache and goatee are aflame.

> His hair streams upward, marked
> In the middle with a half-vajra,
> With Guru Akshobhya in its center.

It is said that 21,000 hairs stream upward. You should visualize the half-vajra in the center of the hair, tying it up. The vajra is hollow in the middle, and the guru in the form of dark blue Akshobhya sits there, naked except for bone ornaments.

> His first right hand holds a nine-pronged vajra;
> His middle one aims a five-pronged vajra in the ten directions.
> His first left hand holds a mound of fire;
> The middle one holds a trident khatvanga.
> His last hands roll the sumeru kilaya.

The purpose of the nine prongs is to establish the realization of the nine bhumis, while the five prongs are for eliminating the five poisons.

The nine-pronged vajra is turned upward, while the five-pronged (vajra) moves around in the ten directions. Of his other hands, one holds a mass of fire like a heap. Another hand holds a trident khatvanga. The mound of fire heap has five points of flames to consume the five poisons, while the three points on the khatvanga are to pierce the three poisons. His main two arms are in front of his heart, where he holds a phurba dagger the size of Mount Sumeru. Since this dagger is known as a sumeru kilaya, some thangka painters depict the top of the handle in the shape of Mount Sumeru, but as Dilgo Khyentse personally told me, that is a big mistake. However, some lamas mistakenly assume such is the case. The Kilaya tantras also state that this means the dagger is as large as Mount Sumeru.

There are three main Kilaya mandalas: The root mandala is yourself in the form of Vajrakilaya; the wrathful mandala is the ten wrathful deities, which surround you; and the substance mandala is the kilaya dagger you hold in your hands.

With vajra-jewel wings outspread,§

The right wing is made of vajras and the left wing is made of jewels. They are fully spread out. I have seen some thangkas in which the wings have the vajras and jewels only at the very tips. However, that is incorrect. The entire wing is made from vajras and jewels, with the very top having feathers like a bird.

He wears an elephant and human skin above,§
And a tiger skin as a skirt.§
Wearing the threefold head garland,§
His head is adorned with five dry skulls,§
Each with jeweled points.§

Ornamented with wreaths of five classes of snakes,§
He is smeared with blood, fat, and ashes§
And wears the six bone ornaments and so forth;§
Thus, the tenfold glorious attire is complete on his body.§
His four legs are poised in the dancing posture.§

His upper garments are made from elephant and human skins, and his skirt is made from a tiger skin. He has three belts of decapitated heads wrapped around his torso like a bandolier. One is made of fresh heads, one of old rotting heads, and the other is made of skulls.

Together with the other ornaments, he wears the ten glorious ornaments of a heruka. These are made from the various things he acquired after subjugating Rudra. There are variations to this list, such as the eightfold charnel ground attire, to which are added the wings and the mass of fire, but I recommend following Karmey Khenpo's version.

He is standing with one leg stretched out slightly in front of the other. This is somewhat like a standing version of the seated playful royal posture.

> On his lap is the consort of union,§
> The dark blue, blazing Diptachakra.§
> Her right hand, with a blue lotus, embraces the lord,§
> And her left proffers a skull cup of blood.§
> She is endowed with the expressions of a fully bloomed maiden.§
> She wears the five mudra ornaments.§
> Her left leg, bent, embraces the waist of the lord,§
> And with her right leg extended, they are joined in great bliss.§

His consort, Diptachakra, is on his lap. She is dark blue and blazes. Her right hand embraces him while holding a blue lotus. In some versions, she is holding a khatvanga instead. The *Zabdun Phurba* doesn't mention it in the visualization, but the praises say she is holding one. She is endowed with *expressions of a fully bloomed maiden.*§ In other words, she has full breasts and a fully developed secret place. She is almost bare except for the five mudra ornaments, which are five different types of bone jewelry. Her bent left leg embraces Vajrakilaya around the waist. She stands with the right leg extended, and they are joined in great bliss. It isn't mentioned here explicitly, but actually she also has a leopard skin skirt.

> At the top of his head are OM HUNG TRAM HRIH AH,§
> Possessing the nature of the five wisdoms.§

The three places, marked with OM AH HUNG,
Are blessed as body, speech, and mind.

At the top of his head are the syllables OM HUNG TRAM HRIH AH, which are inside small skulls. Potentially complicating the visualization, a jewel point is on the top of his head and something with the wrathful deity is below that, which refers to his possessing the nature of the five wisdoms, symbolized by the lines, *His head is adorned with five dry skulls,* *Each with jeweled points.*

He is also marked in his three places with the syllables for body, speech, and mind: OM AH HUNG. This means we can visualize the three forms of deities in a more elaborate style, the three emblems in a medium-level visualization, and the three syllables in a condensed version. In this way, he is blessed with body, speech, and mind.

From the letter HUNG at the secret place of the lord,
A vajra appears, marked with HUNG in its center.
From the letter BAM in the secret space of the consort,
A sun appears, marked with ANG in her lotus.
They sport in the space of great bliss.

In the center of the male figure's secret place is the syllable HUNG. The female deity has the BAM syllable. At the tip, meaning inside, is the AM (ANG) syllable. According to Karmey Khenpo, the HUNG and the AM are touching. In this way, *They sport in the space of great bliss.*

His body hairs are half-vajras,
And he wears an armor of crossed-vajras.
Kilaya tsa-tsas shoot out like stars.

Every single hair on Vajrakilaya's body is a half-vajra, and each of these also sends out sparks in all directions, just like shooting stars. Most wrathful deities have armor that's interwoven and sends out tiny Vajrakilaya figures, like shooting stars.

In his heart center, amidst a dome of light,
Upon a seat of lotus, sun, and moon,

Powerful Transformation

Is the wisdom-being, Vajrasattva.⁰
White and luminous, holding a vajra and bell,⁰
He embraces Atopa, who is holding a knife and skull.⁰
He is seated cross-legged, and within his life-sphere,⁰
Upon a jewel octagon, sun, and moon,⁰
Is a blue vajra with a deep blue HUNG,⁰
Resting upon a sun in its center,⁰
Around which are the self-resounding nine syllables.⁰
Immense light rays radiate from them,⁰
Making pleasing offerings to the body, speech, and mind⁰
Of all the victorious ones of the ten directions.⁰

Up to this point, we've been talking about the development stage of the body aspect. Now we come to what is inside his heart center; it's like a dome of blue light. In Tibet, we didn't have any blue tents, but they are quite common here in the West. This one has eight sides, so it's an octahedron. Inside of this is a lotus flower with sun and moon discs upon it. On this sits Vajrakilaya's wisdom-being, Vajrasattva. Luminous and white, he holds a vajra and bell and embraces Atopa, who holds a knife and skull. This is the typical depiction of Vajrasattva in union with his consort. Vajrasattva is sitting cross-legged, his consort is not sitting in full cross-legged position

Within Vajrasattva's life-sphere (inside his heart center) is a jewel octagon, which has a tip on the top and bottom and eight facets. Inside of that are sun and moon discs, on which a blue five-pronged vajra rests. In the center of the vajra is a sun disc, on which stands a deep blue HUNG. This is surrounded by the syllables of the mantra OM BENZA KILI KILAYA HUNG PHAT, each resounding on its own (not the long mantra). The vajra is the same size as the first segment of your thumb, about one inch. The sun disc is the size of a pea split in half. The HUNG letter on top of the half split-pea sun disc is the same size as a grain of barley. The nine syllables OM BENZA KILI KILAYA HUNG PHAT are as fine as if they were written with a single hair. Each syllable resounds with its individual sound. The immeasurable light rays emitted by the syllables shine in all directions, making offerings that are pleasing to the body, speech, and mind of all the buddhas in the ten directions.

All the blessings of the body, speech, and mind§
Are invited as white OM, red AH, and blue HUNG,§
In an immeasurable amount.§
As they dissolve into my three places,§
I obtain the empowerments, blessings, and siddhis.§

All the blessings of the buddhas' body, speech, and mind come back in innumerable forms of OM, AH, and HUNG in the three colors. They dissolve into your three places of heart, throat, and forehead. We imagine that they dissolve into the white OM, red AH, and blue HUNG at our three places. In this way we absorb and are blessed with all the empowerments, blessings, and siddhis of the buddhas' body, speech, and mind.

The sugatas and gurus are pleased;§
Breaches with dharma brothers and sisters are amended;§
Grudges of dakinis and dharmapalas are cleared;§
All the drekpas are brought to action;§
Maras and samaya-breakers are reduced to dust;§
And all the obscurations of beings' three gates are purified.§

Again the light radiates out, making offerings to all the sugatas and masters. Again rays of light stream out, touching all your dharma brothers and sisters and purifying their broken samaya vows. Your dharma brothers and sisters are those with whom you have received empowerments, explanations of tantras, and so forth. This mends any breaches of samaya with them. Again rays of light stream out, clearing any debts or grudges with the dakinis and dharma protectors. This means any samaya breaches that are held by the dakinis and dharma protectors are cleared. Again rays of light stream out, making the eight classes of drekpas get into line and carry out the activities. Again rays of light radiate out, eliminating all the mara demons and samaya violators. In other words, when the light rays touch the maras and samaya violators, they scatter and disappear, just like blowing on a heap of dust. By radiating to all the sentient beings in the three realms of samsara, the rays purify and totally remove their obscurations, negative karma, and deluded way of perceiving.

Powerful Transformation

All sights are the form of deities,
All sounds are the sound of mantra,
And thoughts are visualized as the display of wisdom.

The essence of your mind should be regarded
As Vajrakumara himself.

OM VAJRA KILI KILAYA SARVA BIGHANEN BAM HUNG PHAT

Thus recite.

We chant the eighteen-syllable mantra written here. Sometimes three mantras are mentioned: a nine-syllable mantra for approach; the above eighteen syllables for accomplishment; and another, called the Marayama, for enacting activities. There is also another in which the approach, accomplishment, and activities are all combined into one. To have all of them complete is quite difficult, in that it is difficult to find a terma text that has all the mantras together in one. I'm not sure why this is. Perhaps some instructions are kept secret for some reason. In any case, it is rare to find all of them in one text. Even the extensive *Zabdun Phurba, The Kilaya of the Sevenfold Profundity*, does not have an in-depth visualization of the simple recitation practice, despite being quite detailed when it comes to the lower activities.

For the meaning of the eighteen-syllable mantra, you should rely on Karmey Khenpo's explanation. Whatever the case, this was the guidance in the speech aspect of recitation. Most importantly, you should regard the essence of your mind as Vajrakumara himself. That is the meditation state itself, though I do not really know anything about it and so I am not going to try to explain.

Offer torma in the session breaks.
Visualize the glorious torma
To be the deity and receive the empowerments.
Begin by offering the flower.

Offering the flower actually means performing a mandala offering. Later in the text, there is a torma offering. According to the Tersar, after having done the mantra recitation in daily practice, you immediately make the torma offering and then proceed to the self-initiation. Self-initiation is only done in retreat or similar circumstances, not otherwise.

> Guru Glorious Heruka,⁞
> Vajrakumara, lord and consort,⁞
> Please bestow the blessings upon me⁞
> And grant the supreme empowerment of body, speech, and mind.⁞
>
> Thus supplicate and visualize yourself as the deity.⁞
>
> From the three places of the deity, the torma,⁞
> Three rays of white, red, and blue light stream out.⁞
> As they dissolve into my three places,⁞
> All the obscurations of the three gates are purified,⁞
> And the empowerments of body, speech, and mind are obtained.⁞

The torma is made in a particular shape, according to the tradition. But when relating to the torma, you should regard it as Vajrakilaya with consort, surrounded by the ten wrathful ones with their consorts, the twenty tratap and the four gatekeepers and the twenty-one supreme sons, all in completeness. The torma is regarded as the four notions. In this case, it is the notion of being the deity. Visualize that at the three places of the torma, which represents the deities, rays of white, red, and blue light radiate. When the light dissolves into your three places, *All the obscurations of the three gates are purified*⁞. This refers to your body, speech, and mind and to obtaining the empowerments of body, speech, and mind.

According to the empowerment explanation, when receiving the white rays of light, you imagine that Varjrakilaya emits countless small bodily forms of the wrathful deities, which enter into your own forehead (you being in the form of Vajrakilaya as well), purifying all obscurations and negative karma committed with bodily actions in the past. By doing so, you receive the blessings and empowerments and siddhis of Vajrakilaya's body. When receiving the red light from Vajrakilaya through the throat center, again countless tiny forms of Vajrakilaya enter your body, purifying the negative karmic actions committed with your voice and cleansing all the obscurations of your voice, such as muteness, stuttering, hesitant speech, and feeble voice. At the same time, you receive the siddhi for Vajrakilaya's speech. Receiving the blue ray of light from Vajrakilaya's mind into your own heart center purifies all negative karma produced on a mental level throughout countless lifetimes until now, all obscurations, and so forth—as well as fainting, insanity, and other mental disorders. Thus, you obtain the siddhi of Vajrakilaya's mind.

Then you imagine that all of the deities represented by the torma—Vajrakilaya and all the surrounding deities—dissolve down into you, as Vajrakilaya, through the crown of your head. When conferring the empowerment of the self-initiation there is a chant in which you call upon each master of the lineage for their blessings, accomplishments, and so forth. All of them in totality become indivisible from your own stream of being.

The chant for this is:

HUNG!
The torma vessel is the blazing space of the dark blue triangle.
The torma essence is the great Glorious Heruka.
Bhagavan Vajrakumara, king of the wrathful,
With supreme consort, Tara Diptachakra,
Mara tamers, ten dancing wrathful ones and consorts,
Supreme sons and all gatekeepers and protectors,

Open the gate of your powerful samaya now,
And bestow upon my body the majestic, supreme body empowerment.
Clear away physical sickness, negative forces, evil deeds, and obscurations.
Make me accomplished in the rainbow body vajra form.

Bestow upon my speech the supreme empowerment of Brahma's voice.
Clear away speech obscurations, stuttering, and muteness.
Please grant the siddhi of the power of wrathful mantras.
Bestow upon my mind the supreme mind empowerment of simplicity.
Pacify mental obscurations, insanity, strokes, and illness,

And grant the siddhi of the mind of great bliss.˶
Moreover, avert sorcery and evil spells,˶
Annihilate viciousness and ill-will,˶
And increase life, merit, splendor, and wealth.˶

Attach at the end of the mantra˶

KAYA VAKA CHITTA SARVA SIDDHI PHALA ABHIKHENTSA HOH˶

Thus receive the empowerment.˶

Now we come to the torma offering. In the first section, we consecrate the torma by turning it into nectar.

For the torma offering, say˶

RAM YAM KHAM burns, scatters, and washes away the torma.˶
From the state of emptiness, upon wind, fire, and a skull-stand,˶
A vast and extensive skull cup manifests from BHRUM.˶
Inside it, the five meats appear from GO KU DA HA NA,˶
And the five nectars flow from BI MU MA RA SHU.˶
The lid is a sun and moon marked with a vajra.˶
By the joining of fire and wind, the nectar melts and boils.˶
The steam gathers all the essences of samsara and nirvana.˶
They become the forms of the five families of lords and
    consorts, united in great bliss.˶
Together with the lid, they melt into bodhichitta.˶
Samaya and wisdom mingle indivisibly as nectar.˶
An offering cloud of desirable objects fills the sky.˶
OM AH HUNG HOH˶

Raising the right hand and pointing the left,˶
Consecrate with the mudra of joined thumb and finger.˶

Here, while reciting RAM YAM KHAM, visualize that the vajra flames, wind, and torrent purify the torma by burning, scattering, and washing it away. Then visualize that from the state of emptiness, a skull vessel resting on a stand appears. The skull cup is as vast as space, and beneath it are wind and fire. Inside of it, the five meats appear from the five syllables GO KU DA HA NA and the five nectars arise from BI MU MA RA SHU. These fill the skull cup, on top of which is a lid made of a sun and moon with a vajra handle. The wind fans the flames heating the contents of the skull cup until they begin to boil and steam rises up. This steam gathers and summons all the essential nectars from all samsaric and nirvanic states, which then become the five male and five female buddhas, who are joined in union. The bodhichitta streams that emerge from the five male and female buddhas also dissolve into the big melting pot. At the end, in the state of great bliss, they dissolve into the nectar of bodhichitta together with the lid made of sun, moon, and vajra. In this way, the samaya being and the wisdom being are indivisibly mingled into a nectar that can emit infinite cloudbanks of desirable objects and sense pleasures that fill the sky. While visualizing this, chant OM AH HUNG HOH three times with a particular mudra and then perform the garuda mudra, according to the Chokling tradition. *Raising* and *pointing* actually refer to the same gesture that you do with both hands. Mindrolling style is immediately one mudra (garuda).

This is like preparing a meal before throwing a party. Now that the torma offering is ready, you invite the guests to join you.

HUNG:
From the palace of dharmadhatu,
Bhagavan Vajrakumara,
With your retinue of protectors and pledge-holders,
Please bestow the empowerments and siddhis,

In order that I may accomplish the Kilaya of existence.
Wrathful Wisdom, please come.
Wrathful Wisdom, having now arrived,
Manifest the signs and marks
And bestow the accomplishment of Kilaya.
VAJRA SAMA DZAH

Powerful Transformation

This is quite easy to understand. From yourself as the great Glorious Vajrakilaya, rays of light stream into all directions, as you request Vajrakilaya to manifest from the *palace of dharmadhatu*, together with his retinue of protectors and pledge-holders, who are mainly the twelve types that carry out the activities of Vajrakilaya. You ask them to approach and bestow empowerments and siddhis. You perform another mudra, and if you have musical instruments, you should play them now.

At this point, you should imagine that all the guests of the seventy-five-fold mandala of Vajrakilaya are present in the sky before you.

> HUNG
> This sacred and supreme offering
> Radiates the light rays of the five wisdoms,
> Fully adorned with the five desirable objects.
> As your heart-samaya, accept these as you please.
>
> OM SHRI VAJRA KUMARA DHARMA PALA SAPARIVARA
> PUSHPE DHUPE ALOKE GANDHE NAIVIDYA SHABDA PRATICCHAYE SVAHA
> MAHA PANCHA AMRITA KHARAM KHAHI
> MAHA RAKTA KHARAM KHAHI
> OM VAJRA KILI KILAYA SAPARIVARA IDAM BALING GRIHANANTU
> MAMA SARVA SIDDHI MEM PRAYACCHA
> OM VAJRA KILI KILAYA DHARMA PALA SAPARIVARA
> IDAM BALINGTA KHA KHA KHAHI KHAHI

These are the words for the offerings. This mantra incorporates the traditional offerings—from flowers to music in the second line—and then has one line each for amrita, rakta, and the main torma offering. We imagine that all the deities enjoy the torma nectar we have consecrated. As a ray of light extends from their tongues to the nectar, they absorb this essential liquid just like we drink soda (with a straw). At the same time, you perform the mudra and snap your fingers, first for the wisdom beings and then for the surrounding retinue.

KHA KHA KHAHI KHAHI means "please have, please have."

After they have received the torma offering, you offer praise:

HUNG:
Skillfully acting for the sake of beings,
Through love and compassion you tame whoever needs help
And perfect the activities of the buddhas.
To all Kilaya Activity deities, I prostrate and offer praise.

Having offered the torma and uttered praise, you call upon the guests, in this case asking them to carry out specific activities.

HUNG:
From the uncontrived space of suchness beyond constructs,
Manifests the blazing form of spontaneously present great bliss,
Bhagavan great Glorious Vajrakumara,
With the supreme consort, Tara Diptachakra.
All knowledge-holders of Vajrakilaya,
The ten wrathful ones, lords and consorts, hosts of devourers and slayers,
Twenty-one supreme sons, four female wrathful gatekeepers,
Hosts of shvanas, sovereigns, bhumipatis, and great beings,
Together with the ocean of Kilaya protectors and pledge-holders,

This verse comprises those to whom your request is directed. You call them by name. Next you make your request:

Manifest here in form, from invisible space.
Accept the samaya substances of outer, inner, and secret offerings,
And the offerings of amrita, rakta, and torma.
For all of us, masters and disciples, patrons and recipients, together with our retinues,
Protect our three gates as well as our riches;
Bestow the siddhis of body, speech, and mind;
Pacify all illnesses, negative forces, and obstacles;
Increase our life spans, merit, glory, and riches;

Magnetize the three realms and the three existences;༔
Perform the activity of reducing animosity and obstructing forces to dust.༔
Turn away all black magic and evil spells,༔
And make auspicious goodness manifest.༔

Thus entreat.༔

First you ask them to receive the offerings and then you request their activities. *All of us, masters and disciples, patrons and recipients,* means all your benefactors and so forth together with their followers and retinues. *Protect our three gates* refers to body, speech, and mind as well as our riches and belongings. The remaining list of petitions includes all four types of activities.

Dissolve the wisdom beings into yourself.༔
Let the loka beings leave to their own places.༔

After this, you dissolve the wisdom beings, who are present in the sky before you, into yourself and ask their retinue of mundane divinities to return to their own places.

Next, the verses state the results of doing this practice,

Through this, all obstacles will be pacified༔
And all wishes will be fulfilled.༔
Therefore, exert yourself in this.༔
This profound oral instruction༔
Is concealed for the sake of future times.༔
May it meet with the person of right karma.༔

Having such virtues, therefore exert yourself in this practice. *This profound oral instruction༔ is concealed for the sake of future times.*༔ Guru Padmasambhava said this. *The person of right karma* refers to the tertön, in this case Chokgyur Lingpa.

SAMAYA GYA GYA༔

The incarnated tertön Chokgyur Dechen Lingpa removed this from the Tsari-like Jewel Rock (Tsadra Rinchen Drak) and established it in writing at the upper retreat of Künzang Dechen Ösel Ling. Padma Gargyi Wangchuk (Jamgön Kongtrül Lodrö Thaye) then wrote it down. May virtuous goodness increase.[8]

When you do this in the solka style of practice, first do the supplication to the lineage masters written by Wangchuk Dorje. Then do the main sadhana, beginning with refuge and bodhichitta and then the visualization. Next, for the recitation, you chant the mantra one hundred times. Then skip the self-initiation and go straight to the torma offering, after which you do the requests. If you have petitions for the dharma protectors, you do them next.

According to Tulku Urgyen's tradition, when you do extensive petitions to the dharma protectors, you use the *Sungma Chitor*. We (Neten Gon) use the *Damchen Chitor*. These texts have their own offerings and praises and dedication at the end. But if you just do the Lama Yidam and Tseringma chants to the dharma protectors, then you should conclude using what is found at the end of the feast text, which includes the offerings and praises, dissolution and re-emergence, dedication, and verses of auspiciousness, and so forth. This is not found in the *Sangtik Phurba* itself, but in another text entitled the *Lungluk Phurba*. Jamgön Kongtrül inserted it here, so that is the tradition.

If you do the *Sungma Chitor*, it has its own conclusion at the end, including the verse of auspiciousness. So you don't need to bring it in from elsewhere.

Phurba Protector

Phurba Mandala

Questions and Answers

Question: How do we organize the feast?

Rinpoche: It is okay to combine the feast text with the terma root text. Jamgön Kongtrül himself said so. There is also an arrangement for this Phurba text put together by Wangchuk Dorje. You can choose either one to use with the feast text. I myself prefer Wangchuk Dorje's when performing the feast. However, when not performing the tsok, just use the terma root text itself. When making a feast offering, you need the various offerings, such as the gektor and different things that can be done all together in Wangchuk Dorje's text. If you just use the terma root text itself, then you don't have to prepare a torma; you can use a biscuit or something like that. In the monastery, as part of the daily rituals, the monks use the terma root text at the time of enjoining the protectors to do their activity.

When Chokgyur Lingpa was alive, at first he would just use the *Kunchok Chidu* terma as the framework for the offerings to the dharma protector. But on the second of his four trips to the Derge area, he revealed this terma up at Tsadra Rinchen Drak, and from then on he used it instead. He asked Jamyang Khyentse how to do the solka for the dharma protectors and he was told to use the Mindrolling style of the *Damchen Chitor*, while adding in some of the protectors for the Tersar. Chokgyur Lingpa then asked Jamgön Kongtrül to write something for that. So there is the Six-Armed Mahakala, Lekye Shinje, Tseringma, Lutsen Barwa Pundon, the Seven Brothers, and Shona. Altogether, they comprise the *Damchen Chitor, The General Torma for the Vow-Holders,* written by Jamgön Kongtrül. The Mindrolling style only contains nine. This is how *Damchen Chitor* was created. Some years after Chokgyur Lingpa passed away, Karmey Khenpo wrote the *Sungma Chitor*. He first wrote an extensive one called the *Ngodrub Gyatso, Ocean of Siddhi,* which combines all the protectors of the Chokling Tersar. Then I heard he got a scolding from Jamgön Kongtrül, who thought some of the protectors were a bit too tough to just be passed around like that, so it was inappropriate. So he made an abbreviated form, which is known as the *Sungma Chitor, The General Torma for the Guardians.* Mindrolling style has both an extensive and an abbreviated version as well, the abbreviated being the *Damchen Chitor.* So for the Chokling tradition, we have the extensive *Ocean of Siddhi* and the abbreviated *General Torma for the Protectors.* This is how the tradition slowly took form.

In the beginning, Chokgyur Lingpa was just by himself. But when he reached the age of twenty-eight or twenty-nine, his fame spread. Even before that, when he went up to see Jamgön Kongtrül for the first time at Tsadra Rinchen Drak, he was known as Kyater; he dressed as a simple monk and was alone. He did, however, already have a good reputation for doing pujas that were beneficial. Nonetheless, the word spread that when inviting Kyater to perform a puja at one's house, it wasn't necessary to send a horse, as people would have done when inviting more celebrated lamas. So, in his early days, Chokgyur Lingpa would just walk.

From the age of twenty-eight until he died in his forties, his fame continued to spread. At the time of his death, he had large monasteries with congregations of monks and so forth.

At the beginning, he was a Drukpa Kagyü monk, and his main practice was *Konchok Chidu.* After discovering the *Sangtik Phurba,* he used it, because before making an offering to the dharma protectors, you need to do a yidam practice. Since then, the tradition for using the *Sangtik Phurba* for that has been unbroken.

When Chokgyur Lingpa performed his first drubchen, there were only twelve participants, including himself and some lamas and monks. During his short life, he performed more than fifty drubchens. If you include the shorter drubchö and other extensive rituals, he probably performed more than one hundred. He didn't have only one monastery either but three: Kela, Neten, and Karma Gon. Now there are more than one hundred associated monasteries, but not in the past.

The concluding verses here, which Tulku Urgyen Rinpoche suggested, come from the end of the feast offering. But before that, just after finishing the torma offering and making the request, you go back and repeat the offering and praises once more. Then you chant the end of the feast offering. But if you do extensive chants to the dharma protectors, such as the *General Torma Offering to the Protectors,* then you don't need to chant those concluding verses, for they are included. However, if you are doing the abbreviated chants to the dharma protectors, then you must include these concluding verses.

Question: When chanting the lines at the beginning for the three samadhis, should we visualize a blue sphere becoming the letter HUNG?

Rinpoche: Actually, the HUNG is the blue sphere, as it glows with light in the shape of a sphere. In his commentary, Karmey Khenpo gives a detailed explanation of the meaning of the color and so forth. He shows off his erudition and scholarship. I wondered why he did that, but it likely came from his habit of standing up and giving a lecture to a large congregation of monks, when it was necessary to show off a bit. It's often like that; when something is a bit difficult to understand, then a learned person will stir up a lot of quotations from various sources, in order to clarify certain points. If it were easy to understand, you couldn't take people for a ride like that. Unless you say something to clarify those three sentences at the beginning, *Vajra-wrath...,* they are not so easy to understand. If it had a form with face and arms, then it would be more tangible and easier to understand. Later, in Tibet, I saw another version of this text by Karmey Khenpo, in which he hadn't added this stuff. So there are different handwritten notes in existence.

At the end of the year, at Ka-Nying Shedrub Ling monastery, they perform the Gutor ceremonies, where they throw big tormas as a sort of exorcism. This is done twice, first as Dorje Phurba and then as Dorje Shonnu. However, in Tibet I once found a small note by Chokgyur Lingpa, which stated that Dorje Phurba doesn't need to throw anything. Since Shonnu is already his wrathful manifestation, the deity himself doesn't need to carry anything out personally, which is quite an interesting concept. It is quite appropriate, but nobody seems to follow this advice, so there is no tradition to do it that way.

Question: What color is the jewel octagon?

Rinpoche: The jewel octagon is a different color than the deep blue dome of light. The jewel is translated as a lapis, but I am not sure that is actually the case. It is said that it has a slightly greenish hue to it. Whatever the case, the samadhi being is very tiny, and in the pith instructions in the Kilaya tradition, the samadhi being is very vital. In the tradition based on the *Zabdun Phurba,* which is more detailed, it states that outside the octagon is another tiny, tiny deity, who is Hayagriva standing on a god; he is like a body guard.

Question: Does the dome of light have eight sides like the eight-sided jewel?

Rinpoche: The dome definitely has eight sides as well. Back in Tibet where I grew up, the tents had lots of different tethers extending in all directions, but this kind of tent or dome doesn't have any ropes; it stands up by itself. In those days, if anybody described a tent without ropes, nobody would understand what they were talking about or be able to picture it in their minds.

Tersar Sangtik Phurba Torma front

Tersar Sangtik Phurba Torma back

Vajrasattva Practice

The Aspiration of Vajrasattva

EXTRACTED FROM *Vajrasattva's Root Tantra, Heart Bindu*

Ema, marvellous and wonderful Dharma.
Everything is manifest from the nonarising.
Everything ceases in the unceasing.
I am the self-existing buddha.

One ground, two paths, and one fruition
Are the magical display of knowledge and ignorance.
The buddha is within,
Yet sentient beings do not recognize it.
Therefore, I feel compassion.

Through this unexcelled magic of mantra,
Of dharmata, skillful means, and coincidence,
May the aspiration of Vajrasattva
And the unimpeded dharmakaya of primordial purity
Be fully accomplished.

Vajrasattva Yabyum

Essence of Blessings

The Lineage Supplication from the Sangtik Nyingpo Trilogy

The Fifteenth Karmapa, Khakyab Dorje

> Chöku kunzang longku dorje sem
> Tulku tragtung rig-nga garab je
> Dorje hung dzey prabha hasti la
> Solwa debso jinlob ngödrub tsol

I supplicate dharmakaya Samantabhadra,
Sambhogakaya Vajrasattva,
And nirmanakaya Garab Dorje, Dorje Hungkara, and Prabhahasti;
Please bestow blessings and accomplishments.

> Kyilkor khyabdag dorje tötreng tsal
> Bairo tsana yeshe tsogyal yum
> Terchen lama pema garwang tsal
> Solwa debso jinlob ngödrub tsol

I supplicate Dorje Tötreng Tsal, lord of the mandala,
Vairochana, Yeshe Tsogyal,
And the great tertön Pema Garwang Tsal;
Please bestow blessings and accomplishments.

> Rigkun dagpo chomden dorje sem
> Demchog drubtsö benza heruka
> Barchey dudul dorje phurpey lhar
> Solwa debso jinlob ngödrub tsol

Powerful Transformation

I supplicate Vajrasattva, the victorious lord of all families,
Sovereign in accomplishing the Vajra Heruka of supreme bliss,
And Vajrakilaya, tamer of obstacle-creating demons;
Please bestow blessings and accomplishments.

> Ngödrub kuntsol masing khandro dang
> Trinley lhundrub damchen gyatsö dey
> Damtsig jechö tersung tsogchey la
> Solwa debso jinlob ngödrub tsol

I supplicate the mother and sister dakinis, who bestow the siddhis,
The ocean of assemblies of those bound by oath, who spontaneously fulfill the activities,
And the treasure guardians, who oversee the samayas;
Please bestow blessings and accomplishments.

> Kyepa yibkyi naljor gyedu gyur
> Ngagkyi dradang dorje nadar drub
> Dechen tigdzin khakyab korlor sey
> Chogdrel lodey gopang ngöngyur shog

May I master the development stage of form-yoga.
May my intonation of mantra become the vajra-sound.
May I awaken to the all-pervading and continuous blissful samadhi
And realize the impartial state beyond concepts.

• • •

In response to Karma Damchö Paldrub, a yogin of the two stages, this was composed by the one who is renowned as the fifteenth in the succession of Karmapas.[20]

---

20 Khakyab Dorje. Guru Rinpoche predicted the fifteenth Karmapa to be one of the fourteen main holders of the terma teachings of Chokgyur Lingpa.

The Practice of the Single Form of Vajrasattva:

According to the Cycle of Sangtik Nyingpo:

Chokgyur Lingpa

Namo:

    Dagsog semchen dugngal droldön du:
    Jangchub bardu kyabsu zungwai ney:
    Lama dorje sempa kunchog sum:
    Yidam khandrö tsogla kyabsu chi:

NAMO:
In order to liberate myself and all sentient beings from suffering,:
I take refuge in Guru Vajrasattva, the Three Jewels, the yidams, and all the dakinis.:
Until enlightenment, I will regard you as my refuge.:

    Dagni ngöngyi gyalwai dzeypa zhin:
    Semchen kungyi dönrab tsönpar ja:
    Semchen magal draldang madröl dröl:
    Semchen ug-yung nyangen degö jug:

Like the buddhas of the past, I will endeavor in the ultimate goal of all beings::
To take those across who have not crossed:
And liberate those who have not been liberated.:
I will encourage beings and establish them in nirvana.:

Dronam deden dugngal drelwa dang༔
Pagpai detob tangnyom laney shog༔

May all beings have happiness and be free from suffering.༔
May they achieve the noble bliss and dwell in equanimity.༔

Chokchui gyalwa sechey dirjön la༔
Pogyur drelmey longdu zhugsu sol༔
Yeney namdag ngangdu chagtsal lo༔
Chönyi namröl chötrin gyatsö chö༔

Buddhas and bodhisattvas of the ten directions,༔
Please come and remain in this expanse that is free from separation and change.༔
I salute you within the primordially pure nature༔
And make offerings as ocean-like clouds, the play of dharmata.༔

Marig digpey legyi tollo shag༔
Ying-rig dudrel mela yirang ngo༔
Khyabdal choglhung drelwey chökhor kor༔
Dusum tagpar nyangen midey zhug༔
Mikmey getsog khanyam drola ngo༔
Dorje sempey gopang tobpar shog༔

I openly admit my misdeeds and ignorance༔
And rejoice in the fact that space and awareness never meet nor part.༔
Please turn the all-pervading and impartial wheel of the Dharma༔
And remain constantly throughout the three times without decline.༔
I dedicate all my nonconceptual merit to beings as numerous as the sky is vast,༔
So that they may attain the state of Vajrasattva.༔

Powerful Transformation

Homage to Vajrasattva[21]

The yogin who wishes to attain accomplishments should, with a mind firm upon renunciation, go to a retreat place, take refuge in the Three Jewels, arouse the mind set on supreme enlightenment, and be diligent in accumulating merit through the Seven Branches.

>Chönam tamchy tongpa nyi༔
>Dechen ösal nyingjey tsal༔
>Zungjug hung yig karpo ley༔
>Ötrö dorje meyi gur༔
>Nangdu jungwa rirab teng༔

>Everything, including all phenomena, is emptiness.༔
>Great bliss, luminosity, is the play of compassion.༔
>The unity of these is a white letter HUNG,༔
>Which, by radiating light, creates a dome of vajras and flames,༔
>Inside of which are the elements and Mount Sumeru.༔

>Pema dabma tongden ü༔
>Drung ley rinchen zhalye khang༔
>Dal-ü sengtri pema dang༔
>Nyidey tengdu hung yig ni༔
>Dorje hung gi tsenpar sal༔

>Upon these is a thousand-petaled lotus,༔
>In the center of which, the syllable BHRUM becomes a jeweled celestial palace;༔
>In its middle is a lion throne with a lotus, sun, and moon with the syllable HUNG on top;༔
>I imagine it becomes a vajra marked with a HUNG.༔

>Ötrö gyalchö jinlab dü༔
>Drowey ledrib malü jang༔
>Dorje sempey sala kö༔
>Tsurdü yongyur kechig la༔

---

21. The main terma text begins at this point. The lineage supplication was composed by Khakyab Dorje and the refuge, bodhichitta, and Seven Branches were from the general termas of Chokgyur Lingpa.

Light radiates making offerings to the buddhas and gathering
their blessings.༔
It purifies all the karmas and obscurations of beings༔
And establishes them in the state of Vajrasattva.༔
As the light is absorbed back,༔

Rangnyi lama dorje sem༔
Karpo zhalchig zhizhing dzum༔
Utra tortsug rinchen gyen༔
Chagyey dorje tugkar tö༔
Yönpey drilbu kula ten༔
Zhabnyi dorje kyiltrung zhug༔

I am instantly transformed into Guru Vajrasattva.༔
White, with one face, peaceful and smiling.༔
My hair is in a topknot, and I am adorned with jewelry.༔
My right hand holds a vajra at my heart center,༔
My left a bell at my thigh.༔
I am seated with my two legs in vajra posture.༔

Tsenzang pejey tamchey dzog༔
Zidir darchang chöpen dang༔
Töyog meyog dzepar kri༔
Ugyen nyencha gulgyen dang༔
Seymo dodang doshal dang༔
Dubu namkyi lekpar gyen༔

Beautifully dressed in silken scarfs, head band,༔
And upper and lower garments,༔
I am fully adorned with a crown, earrings, necklace,༔
Garlands, rings, and bracelets.༔

Pangdu dorje nyemma kar༔
Chudrug langtso dritö chen༔
Chagya ngachang yabdang tril༔
Öbar longdu lhammer kye༔

On my lap is white Vajratopa,༔
A youthful sixteen-year-old, who holds a curved knife and a
skull cup.༔

Powerful Transformation

Adorned with the five mudras, she embraces me.
I visualize this vividly and clearly, within an expanse of radiant light.

Chiwor om hung tram hrih ah
Yeshe ngayi dagnyi chen
Chidrin nyingar om ah hung
Kusung tugsu jingyi lab

On the crown of my head are OM HUNG TRAM HRIH AH,
The nature of the five wisdoms.
At my forehead, throat, and heart centers are OM AH HUNG,
Giving blessings for body, speech, and mind.

Tugkar pema dawey teng
Dorje karpo tsenga pey
Tewar dawa laney pey
Hung yig taru yigyey kor

Within my heart center, upon a lotus and moon,
Is a bright five-spoked vajra.
In its middle is a moon, upon which the letter HUNG
Is surrounded by the Hundred Syllable mantra.

Özer samey tröpa yi
Digdrib bagchag nedön jang
Desheg namla nyechö bül
Kusung tugkyi jinlab dü
Lama yidam nyepar jey
Checham khandrö tukdam kang

By radiating inconceivable rays of light,
Negative actions, obscurations, tendencies, diseases,
And all evils are purified.
All the sugatas are presented with pleasing offerings.
The blessings of their body, speech, and mind are gathered.
The gurus and yidams are pleased
And the samayas of the family dakinis are mended.

Powerful Transformation

Chökyong sungmey könjang shing༔
Trinley namzhi leyla kül༔
Düdang gegkyi dangsem zhi༔
Drowaey leydrib malü jang༔
Nöchü dorje sempey zhing༔
Lha-ngag yeshe rölpar gyur༔

The grudges of the dharma protectors are cleared,༔
And they are called upon to enact the four activities.༔
The aggressions of Mara and the negative forces are pacified,༔
And all karmas and obscurations of beings are purified.༔
The universe and all beings are turned into the realm of Vajrasattva,༔
Creating a vast display of deities, mantras, and primordial wakefulness.༔

Chant the mantra like the flow of a river.༔

OM VAJRA SATTVA SAMAYA༔ MANU PALAYA༔ VAJRA SATTVA TVENOPA༔ TISHTHA DRIDHO MEBHAVA༔ SUTOSHYO MEBHAVA༔ SUPOSHYO MEBHAVA༔ ANU RAKTO MEBHAVA༔ SARVA SIDDHI ME PRAYACCHA༔ SARVA KARMA SUCHAME༔ CHITTAM SHRE YAM༔ KURU HUNG༔ HA HA HA HA HOH༔ BHAGAVAN༔ SARVA TATHAGATA༔ VAJRA MAME MUNCA༔ VAJRI BHAVA༔ MAHA SAMAYA SATTVA AH༔

By merely reciting this a single time,༔
The five actions with immediate results and obscurations are purified.༔
Even the place of Narak is emptied,༔
And you will be inseparable from Vajrasattva.༔[iv]

Recite remorseful apology:༔

Lama dorje sempa kye༔
Narak dugngel kyabtu sol༔
Digpey tsokla dagnong zhing༔
Gyöpey gönpö drungdu shag༔

Powerful Transformation

Guru Vajrasattva, pay heed!པ
Protect me from the painful Narak!པ
I regret all my negative actions,པ
And with remorse I apologize for them before you.པ

Chiney migyi damchey peyཔ
Gönpo tsangpar tsaldu soཔ
Semchen kungyi döngyi chirཔ
Dorje sempa daggi drubཔ
Kusung tugsu dagjor teyཔ
Lamey sala drangdu solཔ

Since I resolve to never commit them henceforth,པ
May you absolve me, protector!པ
For the sake of all sentient beingsཔ
I will accomplish Vajrasattva.པ
Unite me with your Body, Speech and Mind.པ
Lead me to the unexcelled state!པ

*Dissolve and re-emerge:*པ

Nangsi özhu tendang tenpar timཔ
Sungkhor jungwa zhalyey khangdang triཔ
Ngöpo gyennam yabyum sosor timཔ
Yabyum özhu dorje ngaktreng laཔ
Deyang hung la hung yang nadey barཔ
Denyi mimik kadag ngangla zhagཔ
Laryang dorje sempey kuru langཔ

Appearance and existence melt into lightཔ
And dissolve into the mandala of the deity.པ
The protection circle, the elements, the celestial palace,པ
The throne, and all the attributes and ornamentsཔ
Dissolve one by one into the lord and lady.པ
The lord and lady melt into light,པ
Then into the vajra and mantra chain, which further dissolve
    into HUNG,པ
And HUNG dissolves up to the nada,པ

Which is left in the nongrasping state of primordial purity.
Again I emerge in the form of Vajrasattva.

Hoh
Lamey yeshe lejung wai
Sönam tayey dampa dey
Khanyam semchen malü kun
Dorje sempa tobpar shog

HOH
Through the pure and endless merit
Arising from unexcelled wisdom,
May all beings equal to the sky
Attain the state of Vajrasattva.

Gyurwa mepa ranggi shi
Tagching tenpa dorjey ney
Rangrig yeshe yermey par
Ngönsang gyepey tashi shog

May there be the auspiciousness of true awakening,
Inseparable from the spontaneous awareness-wisdom,
The permanent and firm vajra-abode
Of the changeless nature.

• • •

This terma treasure was recovered from Tsadra Jewel Rock[22] by the great treasure revealer Chokgyur Dechen Lingpa. It was then committed to writing in the upper retreat of Künzang Dechen Ösel Ling by Padma Gargyi Wangchuk (Jamgön Kongtrül Lodrö Thaye). May it increase virtuous goodness.

This Daily Practice of Sangtik Dorsem was re-arranged by Mingyur Dewey Dorje, the fourth incarnation of Tsikey Chokgyur Lingpa at the request of Graham, my late father's American disciple. It was translated into English by Erik Pema Kunsang, with the help of some dharma friends. Edited by Michael Tweed. Phonetics by Graham Sunstein.

---

22 Tsadra Rinchen Drak is the mountain behind Palpung Monastery in Kham. It is called "Tsa-like" because it resembles Tsaritra on Mount Kailash. The retreat house Künzang Dechen Ösel Ling is where Jamgön Kongtrül the First spent most of his life.

The Words of Vajrasattva[23]

An Explanation of the Crucial Points of the Development and Completion Stages for the Single-Mudrā Vajrasattva from the Secret Heart Essence (Sangtik Nyingpo) Cycle

Pema Drimé Lodrö Shyenpen Chökyi Nangwa

Homage to the guru and glorious Vajrasattva!

I shall write down a brief explanation of the visualization stages for the practice of Vajrasattva from the *Secret Heart Essence (Sangtik Nyingpo)* as taught by the supreme Vidyādhara Guru. The explanation contains three parts: I) the preliminaries, II) the main part, and III) the concluding stages.

I. The Preliminaries

The discussion of the preliminaries contains two subsections: A) the preliminaries for engaging in a session and B) the preliminary instructions that make one a fit vessel for the path.

A. The Preliminaries for Engaging in a Session

In a solitary place, sit down on a comfortable seat, upright and in the correct posture, and let your mind rest naturally at ease. Then exhale the stale breath three times from your two nostrils and think that now all

---

23 Most of this commentary was translated by Ani Laura Dainty with sections completed by Ryan Conlon, Lungrik Rabsel, who checked the translation, as did Marcia Dechen Wangmo, and Lama Sean Price, who also cleared up difficult points.

your misdeeds and obscurations are purified. Remembering the altruistic motivation, think, "For the benefit of all sentient beings, I am going to practice the profound path!" Imagine that above the crown of your head is your root guru, who is endowed with the threefold kindness.[v] Confidently trusting that your root guru is the embodiment of all objects of refuge, supplicate them with [prayers, beginning with] *Buddha of the three times, Guru Rinpoche,*§ *Emaho! Dharmakāya Samantabhadra* . . . and so on, completely entrusting yourself to them. Then dissolve the guru into yourself. Be sure to do this at the beginning of every session.

B. The Preliminary Instructions That Make One a Fit Vessel for the Path

It says in the root treasure text, *The yogin who wishes to attain accomplishments should, with a mind firm upon renunciation.*§ Thus, those who wish to attain both the supreme and common accomplishments in this life should first develop renunciation. That is essential. Likewise, the precious Master of Uddiyāna taught, *With intense renunciation, endeavor in accepting and rejecting what concerns cause and effect.*[vi] Therefore, in order to develop renunciation, it is extremely important to reflect again and again on the difficulty of attaining the freedoms and favors, the impermanence of life, and karmic ripening. Meditate on them until they become deeply merged with your mind. The great treasure revealer Vajradhara[vii] stated this repeatedly whenever he gave teachings.

To begin, we go for refuge in the general way and arouse bodhichitta, the root of the Mahāyāna. In the root treasure text it says,

> . . . *go to a retreat place, take refuge in the Three Jewels, arouse the mind set on supreme enlightenment, and be diligent in accumulating merit through the Seven Branches.*§

Thus, placing your trust in the Three Jewels—the objects of refuge that free sentient beings from the terrifying suffering of samsāra, which is like a pit of fire and a nest of poisonous snakes—go for refuge [while visualizing] the refuge objects in whichever way is suitable, elaborate or simplified. Then arouse the precious bodhichitta of aspiration and application and recite, "HOH. Vajra master, glorious buddha," and so forth three times.[viii] While reciting, "May all sentient beings possess happiness[a]" and so on,[ix] meditate on the four immeasurables and then dissolve the field of accumulation into yourself.

I have simply mentioned these parts of the practice as a reminder, assuming that one is already well-trained in them. However, it is important that beginners train fully in the preliminaries, according to *Accomplishing the Guru's Wisdom Mind, Dispeller of All Obstacles* (*Tukdrub Barchey Künsel*), Avalokiteśvara, or other [cycles].

II. The Main Part

This has three subsections, instructions on, A) enlightened body, the mudrā of the development stage, B) enlightened speech, the recitation of mantra, and C) enlightened mind, the suchness of completion stage.

A. Enlightened Body, the Mudrā of the Development Stage

Sit in the sevenfold posture as is generally explained. There are two stages to this part of the practice: 1) pitching the framework of the three samādhis and 2) developing the inseparable samaya-jñāna [samaya-wisdom] maṇḍala.

1. Pitching the Framework of the Three Samādhis

Regarding the first of the three samādhis, the samādhi of suchness, the sādhana reads,

Everything, including all phenomena, is emptiness.[a]

Practicing this means resting the nonexistent mind within a state in which all grasping to subject and object—all external phenomena, perceived objects, and internal phenomena, the aggregates, elements, sense faculties, consciousnesses, and self-grasping—dissolve like a rainbow into the sky, as if they have vanished into space.

It is vital that the functions of purifying, perfecting, and ripening are complete within each samādhi. This being so, the samādhi of suchness cleanses and purifies the death state. By planting the seed for actualizing the dharmakāya, it arranges the circumstances for perfecting the fruition. By laying the ground for the completion stages of the higher paths, where ultimate luminosity dawns in the mind stream, it enables ripening.

Regarding the second of the three samādhis, the all-illuminating samādhi, the sādhana reads,

> Great bliss, luminosity, is the play of compassion.[8]

This samādhi involves training in the understanding that although all beings who have not realized this appear, they are devoid of reality. With the light of great, pervasive illusory compassion, free of grasping towards its illusory object, think, "I will establish them in the state of supreme enlightenment."

This samādhi purifies the intermediate state. It arranges the circumstances for perfecting the samboghakāya fruition. It ripens by laying the ground for the dawning of great compassion in the mind stream, which is the cause for this very luminosity to emerge as the wisdom kaya.

Regarding the third of the three samādhis, the causal samādhi, the sādhana reads,

> The unity of these is a white letter HUNG,[8]

As it says, visualize the white syllable HUNG, unified self-knowing awareness, which appears from within luminosity, as the nature of bliss, clarity, and emptiness. This samādhi purifies the consciousness of the moment of conception. It arranges the circumstances for the fruition of the nirmanakāya, which tames beings according to their needs, to manifest from within the samboghakāya. It lays the ground for manifesting in the form of the wisdom deity in the completion stage.

2. *Developing the Inseparable Samaya-Jñāna Maṇḍala*

This has three subdivisions: a) visualizing the protection circle; b) visualizing the support, the maṇḍala; and c) visualizing the supported, the form of the deity.

a. *Visualizing the Protection Circle*

As it says in the sādhana,

Powerful Transformation

Which, by radiating light, creates a dome of vajras and flames⁕

Visualize that from the causal syllable HUNG, light rays radiate out and form a vajra-ground, encircling wall, and canopy adorned at the top by a half-vajra, which is surrounded by wisdom fire that blazes beyond all dimensions. This purifies the habitual tendencies of entering the womb, part of the birth state. It arranges the circumstances for the fruition of conquering the four māras. It lays the ground for breaking through obstructing factors and errors, regarding the completion stage practice of the nāḍīs, prana, and bindu.

As a side note, supreme practitioners see that all thoughts of nonvirtue, self-interest, attachment to ordinary appearances, and grasping to entities are by nature indivisible and unchanging emptiness and great bliss. Emptiness is vajra-like, and great bliss is like the blaze of fire; therefore, such conceptual thoughts do not arise. For such practitioners, preventing such thoughts from arising is the protection circle. Nevertheless, the manner of visualizing the protection circle as mentioned above is an unsurpassable means for purifying, perfecting, ripening, and so on; as such, it is very important.

b. *Visualizing the Support, the Maṇḍala*[24]
Inside of which are the elements and Mount Sumeru.⁕

Within the protection circle, the causal syllable HUNG radiates out the syllables E, YAM, RAM, KHAM, LAM, and SUM, one on top of the other, from which appear the maṇḍalas of space, wind, fire, water, and earth together with Mount Sumeru.

Upon these is a thousand-petaled lotus.⁕
In the center of which, . . . ⁕

On top of the stacked elements and Mount Sumeru is a lotus with a thousand petals and anthers. On the anthers is a sun disc, in the center of which is a multi-colored crossed vajra with twelve spokes. Visualize this crossed vajra as being blue in the east, yellow in the south, red in the

---

24 See Appendix

west, green in the north, and white in the center. These purify the establishment of the vessel—the five elements, which are the basis for the formation of the universe, and Mount Sumeru.

They arrange the circumstances for the pure lands, in which those who are to awaken will awake. The secret space of the five female buddhas, being perfected in dharmadhātu, represent these pure lands.

In the completion stage, the five elements and Mount Sumeru are the *chakras* and *avadhuti* (central channel) appearing as lotus, sun disc, and crossed vajra—the channels, subtle winds (pranas), and essences.

These then are different ways to interpret the pure realm.

> ... the syllable BHRUM becomes a jeweled celestial palace;

From the causal syllable HUNG on top of the multi-colored vajra, BHRUM emerges and transforms into a celestial palace, square in shape with four doorways and either four or eight vestibules. With a *phyur bu*[25] adorned with a vajra top ornament and so on, it is replete with the attributes of a celestial palace. As the root text says,

> In its middle is a lion throne with a lotus, sun, and moon with the syllable HUNG on top;

Thus, you visualize an eight-petalled lotus, in the center of which is a jeweled throne supported by eight lions, with a lotus and moon seat. The celestial palace purifies the habitual tendencies of craving and grasping to the buildings that sentient beings utilize, and the lotus and moon seat purifies the habitual tendencies of craving and grasping to womb birth and other locations. Visualizing the celestial palace arranges the circumstances for the manifest accomplishment of the fruition: the celestial palace that is the wisdom wheel of natural experience.

At the time of the completion stage, the celestial palace is merely symbolic of bliss, the union of clarity and emptiness of mind, within which the channels, prana, and bindus (essences) are experienced to be of one taste.

---

25 We have left this term in Tibetan because we could not find a proper equivalent in English. It is a raised center part of the roof that covers the skylight.

The lotus seat represents the crown chakra and the moon symbolizes the perfection of bliss—arising as the sixteenth stage of bliss, the reversal of essential fluids reaching their final destination: the crown of the head.

c. Visualizing the Supported, the Form of the Deity

This has two subsections: i) development and ii) consecration.

i. Development

This is the development by means of the threefold ritual. As the root terma says,

Sun and moon with the syllable HUNG on top;

You are Guru Vajrasattva.

The causal syllable HUNG descending onto the seat is the ritual of the seed syllable of enlightened speech. Visualizing the deity's family insignia, a white five-pronged vajra, marked in its center by HUNG is the ritual of the insignia of enlightened mind. Light rays then radiate out from the syllable and gather back, performing the twofold benefit. The syllable then turns into a ball of light. When you utter OM VAJRA SATTVA AH, the ball of light manifests in the form of Vajrasattva.

The ritual of the fully perfected body of the deity purifies the consciousness entering the joined white and red essences in the womb; the subsequent experience of the five stages of gestation[26] that occur as a result of the parent's intercourse; and the merging together of the ovum, semen, and mind followed by the gradual development of the body via the ten winds, wherein the faculties become complete and one is then born. It arranges the circumstance for the fruition of the buddhas manifesting as nirmanakāyas to tame beings according to their needs, by performing the enlightened deeds of entering the womb and being born.

In the context of the completion stage, the seed syllable and hand implement are symbolic of the prana dissolving into the dhūti (channel). The radiating and gathering back of light rays symbolize the empty-bliss that arises from bliss induced through the melting of the elements. The

---

26 Small writing is referring to five periods of gestation marked by the size and feel of the fetus, as explained in the Tibetan medical tradition.

complete body/kāya lays the ground for the accomplishment of the unchanging empty-bliss, co-emergent wisdom body/kāya.

When the text says *guru,* as mentioned in the sādhana above, it is very important to always regard the yidam deity as being the root guru in essence. As taught in the *All-Embodying Precious Tantra of the Early Translations,*

> Compared to meditating on a hundred thousand deities
> For a hundred thousand aeons,
> Simply remembering the guru is better.
> It brings about infinite merit.

Likewise, it says in *Vajra Mirror,*

> Vajrasattva is the chief of the maṇḍala,
> The guru, equal to all buddhas.

You must understand this. On the contrary, if, like some people, you think it is enough to meditate on the precious Master of Uddiyāna and completely forget about the guru who has given you empowerment and pith instructions, you will be distorting one of the most crucial points of the dharma; so, understand this key point.

The treasure revealers meditate in that way, remembering the precious Master of Uddiyāna, because the guru who gives empowerment and pith instructions to the treasure revealers is the precious Master of Uddiyāna himself. However, to apply that approach yourself would be taking things too far. It is taught in all of the sūtras and tantras that the root of all paths rests on devotion to the guru. Therefore, understand that this is a vital point.

Vajrasattva's body is a translucent white. He has one face and is smiling peacefully. His hair is in a topknot and adorned with jewels. In his right hand, he holds a vajra with his index finger and thumb at his heart center. In his left hand, he rests a bell on his thigh. He embraces the consort and is seated with his two legs in vajra posture. He is adorned with the thirty-two excellent marks and the eighty signs. He wears multi-colored silk ribbons (many short ribbons of various colors that drape down the back of his neck) and a dark blue silk scarf that is inlaid with multi-colored strands. He wears a silken headdress, which is dark blue on the right side, where it rises up above his right ear and is red on the left side, where it drapes down below his left ear. These days this is illustrated by silk ribbons around the ears that are drawn draped around the hook formed by the ornamental designs on the crown that rise up above the ears.

His shirt is made of white silk decorated with a golden *ngangri* pattern. Some people explain the ngangri pattern to be drawings (*ri*) of golden geese (*ngang pa*), but this is incorrect. This interpretation confuses the word's general and specific references, like mistaking the wood called *shawa* for the mountain animal called *shawa*. The ngangri pattern referred to here is the pattern also known as *hakori, halori, ngangri, hatsangri*, and so on; it is round and curvy, similar to the shape of leaves on a tree. He is beautifully dressed in a multi-colored silk skirt.

Vajrasattva wears the eight jewel ornaments: a crown made from blossoming golden lotuses filled with jewels; two round, white earrings studded with jewels; a beautiful choker; a medium-length necklace that extends down to his breasts; a long necklace that drapes down below his navel; armbands and bracelets; anklets; and a golden belt. This belt is studded with jewels topped with lattices of jewels and hanging tassels with small silver bells at their ends.

The five silk garments can be enumerated varyingly, according to different traditions. For instance, in the Minling Vajrasattva practice, in addition to the shirt, skirt, headdress, and silk ribbons listed above, the fifth garment is said to be dancing sleeves. These are sleeves at the end of the shirt that extend down to just above the elbows. I also saw that some earlier masters identified the garment called *darkug* as the silk scarf. *The Testament of Songtsen*, a treasure revealed by Drubtob Ngödrub, mentions a dark blue belt that extends down the legs as a short lower garment. This belt is counted as one of the five garments and the dancing sleeves are not included. Some others include a silk chest ribbon and exclude the silk ribbons. Thus, we have many different enumerations and should not get attached to any one particular way.

On his lap is white consort Atopa, a youthful sixteen-year-old. Holding a curved knife and skull cup in her two hands, she is seated in the lotus posture, embracing the lord. Aside from the five bone mudrās and a jewel crown, she is ornament-free and naked.

The six mudrās have the essence of the six pāramitās and the identity of the six families. The crown chakra, associated with concentration, is Akṣhobhya; the choker, representing generosity, is Ratnasambhava; the earrings, symbolizing patience, are Amitābha; the six bangles (armbands, bracelets, and anklets), refer to discipline and Vairocana; the belt, indicating diligence, is Amoghasiddhi; and ash, symbolizing prajñāpāramitā, is Vajrasattva. In this context, since the Bhagavānī is the identity of prajñāpāramitā, and there is no need to seal prajñā with prajñā, the ash is excluded. Thus she is sealed with the five mudrās of skillful means and visualized like that in the midst of light and light rays.

ii. Consecration

This is referred to with the following lines:

> On the crown of my head are OM HUNG TRAM HRIH AH,
> The nature of the five wisdoms.
> At my forehead, throat, and heart centers are OM AH HUNG
> Giving blessings for body, speech, and mind.

Apply the extensive, concise, or middling styles of visualization, with regard to the mudrās of enlightened body, the syllables of enlightened speech, and the hand implements of enlightened mind, according to the context. In order to counteract attachment to ordinary appearances, adopt the pride thinking, "I am glorious Vajrasattva, the embodiment of all victors!" Practice until you gain a deep and steady certainty in the fact that the deity's form has no existence apart from your own awareness expression. Furthermore, Lochen Chöpal Gyatso taught that if you can embody the vivid continuity of divine pride while remaining free from grasping—and thereby come to understand the key point of the innate—this becomes the genuine short-cut path.

Now for training in the recollection of purity. At the time of the ground, self-arising wisdom has never been tainted by faults and flaws and is naturally pure. At the time of the fruition, this self-arising wisdom is freed from all fluctuating, adventitious obscurations. For these reasons, their bodies are white in color.

At the time of the ground, the primordial true nature (dharmatā) is equality, and while the dharmatā nature never wavers from that state, from the perspective of its aspects, there are the two truths. At the time of the fruition, the two accumulations are perfected, or alternatively one can say one is endowed with the wisdom that understands all that exists and the way it exists. Therefore, Vajrasattva has two hands. In both the ground and fruition, the subject is the self-arising five primordial wisdoms of equal taste, and the object is emptiness, free from constructs. In particular, at the time of the fruition, Vajrasattva performs the benefit of beings through skillful means and wisdom, illustrated by the vajra and bell hand implements.

At the time of the ground, in the original natural state, existence and peace are indivisible. At the time of the fruition, by perfecting prajñā and great compassion, one is freed from the extremes of existence and peace. His legs in the vajra posture represent this. Since at the time of the ground, the torment of the afflictions has never tainted the basic nature, and at the time of the fruition, one is freed from such torment, he wears the five silk garments. Since the nature of all virtuous phenomena is fully perfected, his hair is in a topknot. He is adorned with the eight jewel ornaments of reveling in all sense pleasures, as ornaments of primordial wisdom. The lady's curved knife and skull cup symbolize cutting through concepts and sustaining nonconceptual bliss. As the unity of emptiness and compassion, the lord and lady are entwined in union.

Once you have developed experience of clarity, purity, and stability in visualizing the deity in that way, in order to develop your proficiency (*rstal sbyang*) in samādhi, train in visualizing different sizes, sometimes large and sometimes small.

B. Enlightened Speech, Recitation of Mantra

There are three types of recitation: the coarse prana recitation, the subtle vajra recitation, and verbal recitation.

The first is practicing mental recitation, while holding either the vase breath or intermediate breath. The second is reciting the three seed syllables in conjunction with the breath. However, here you should take the verbal recitation of the Hundred Syllables as the principal recitation. For as it says in the main text,

Chant the mantra like the flow of a river.[g]

In Vajrasattva's heart center, upon a lotus and moon disc, is a white five-pronged vajra. In its central hub, upon a moon disc, is a white syllable HUNG, encircled by the Hundred Syllables. The Hundred Syllables face outward and are arranged anti-clockwise, beginning from the front so that the tail of the mantra ends up inside. Even if you visualize Vajrasattva's body as enormous, the letters of the Hundred Syllables should be visualized proportionately. Therefore, it is taught that regardless of size, the end of the mantra should always be inside.

To begin with, write the Hundred Syllables out correctly in white on a black background and look at them until you gain familiarity. Train like that until you feel that the Hundred Syllables appear vividly and clearly as objects of your mind.

When training in visualizing syllables, regarding the syllable A for instance, there are eight levels of clarity and stability, as taught in the *Guhyagarbha Tantra*. These are as follows. Unmoving, unchanging, completely unchanging, and able to transform into anything whatsoever are the four levels of becoming fully stable. Together with that stability, the color white is endowed with the four levels of clarity: clear, bright, lucid, and vivid. One trains in keeping the mind one-pointedly on the letter endowed with these qualities. Also, it is said there to purify attachment to the appearance of experienced objects one should visualize countless numbers of extremely small syllable As emanating out from the A. You should learn about this from the commentary on the *Guhyagarbha Tantra*, *Ornament of the Lord of Secret's Intent*.

As for the recitation of the Hundred Syllables, recite according to the oral instructions of Dharmakari, which are based upon the oral tradition of Lochen Dharmasri.

The lines, *Within my heart center . . . up through . . . a vast display of deities, mantras, and primordial wakefulness*,[8] describe the visualization when reciting the mantra. Understand that here the jñānasattva is the moon disc and HUNG is Vajrasattva's pure essence life-force. You imagine that from the mantra garland of the recited mantra, light rays radiate out, filling space. They make offerings to the victors and their heirs and gather all of the blessings and siddhis in the form of light rays that dissolve back into you. That is the visualization of blessings for one's own benefit. Then imagine that light from Vajrasattva's heart center strikes beings and thereby purifies them of misdeeds and obscurations and establishes them in the state of Vajrasattva, supreme, unchanging great bliss. The light rays are then gathered back and dissolve into the mantra garland in your heart center. That is the recitation of activity for the benefit of others.

In all cases and styles of recitation, you should understand the threefold clarity, the trio of outer, inner, and secret—the clarity of oneself being the samayasattva, the deity being the jñānasattva, and the visualization of radiating out and gathering back between them—and the threefold subtleties when radiating out and gathering back—tiny syllables, hand implements, and bodily forms that comprise the vajra recitation.

During the approach, you open the recitation mansion, and by emanating white light rays out to it, you entreat (the deities) to purify obscurations. Gathering them back so your obscurations are purified, you become a fit vessel for the siddhis. You perform the recitation while imagining that. At the end, you dissolve the mandala back into yourself.

During the close approach, the radiating out and gathering back during the recitation is as follows: By emanating out white light rays, you invoke the jñānasattvas, and by gathering back red light rays, you become a fit vessel for the siddhis.

During the accomplishment, by emanating out red light rays, you invoke the siddhis, and when gathering the light rays back, imagine that you have obtained the siddhis of enlightened body, speech, and mind. In this way, you perform the emanating out and gathering back alternately.

During the great accomplishment recitation, you do not emanate light rays out; you only gather in dark blue light rays, and the siddhis dissolve into the mind streams of the practitioners.

Generally speaking, when performing the emanating out and gathering back in these ways, you can either separate the samayasattvas and jñānasattvas or not. Here, however, since the objects of the emanating out and gathering back are the victors' purelands that pervade space and all sentient beings without discrimination, there is no need to separate the samayasattvas and jñānasattvas. Perform the recitation without parting from the state of the threefold stance of appearances, sounds, and thought movements as deity, mantra, and primordial wisdom.

As for the meaning of the recited mantra, the opening syllable OM is the identity of the vajra body of all sugatas manifest in the form of a letter. It says in the *Vajra Peak*,

Why recite the syllable OM?
For it is the supreme wealth treasure,
Glory, luck, good fortune,
Commitment, and auspiciousness;
Thus, said to be the jewel-holding mantra.

The syllable OM is said to contain eight meanings. From among these, here it means "commitment" and the "supreme treasure of auspiciousness." VAJRA has the nature of prajñā—emptiness, completely untouched by other conditions, constructs, or characteristics. SATTVA means "being" (*sempa*). It refers to the skillful means of great compassion, or, alternatively, unchanging great bliss, the three doors perfected as a unity free of division. As it says in the *Hevajra Tantra*,

VAJRA means indivisible,
SATTVA, lord of the three planes of existence.

Therefore, Vajrasattva is the indivisibility of emptiness and great compassion, great bliss—the equal taste of their unity. During the stained, impure state, this is called "samsara." During the more subtle state, the stages of purifying the stains, it is called the "path," and in the completely stain-free state, it is called "enlightenment." This result of purification, appearing as a reflection for the sake of those to be tamed, is the symbolic Vajrasattva.[27]

SAMAYA,[28][29] within the context of the mantra, refers to the sacred commitments (of Vajrayāna); however, in other contexts, it can also mean "time," among other things. The term *sacred commitments* implies that which is not transgressed, meaning also that the profound secret of Vajrasattva is not transgressed or gone beyond. Adding the AM of the accusa-

---

[27] We are unable to translate the following line, due to corrupt texts; see note 28. The whole text is full of mistakes that we have tried to correct.
[28] Ryan Conlon, Lungrik Rabsel, translated the mantra, and footnotes # 28-53 are his.
[29] This section contains a number of challenges. Although we have verified these passages with Sanskrit pandits in Nepal, many of the interpretations of Sanskrit grammar given here do not match any known explanations. There also appear to be numerous scribal errors. Notes regarding these issues have been provided throughout. Nevertheless, the overall interpretation of the mantra is more or less correct and the accompanying explanation is certainly worth the rather difficult task of translation.

tive case to SAMAYA, the mantra then reads SAMAYAM *anupālay,* MANU PALAY, the latter word being the imperative[30] of the verb "to guard." Thus, the sacred commitments are to be guarded. When joined to the next word, the rules of SANDI *sandhi*[31] change the ANUSVARAM *anusvāra* ṃ into M, making SAMAYA MANU PALAYA *samaya manupālaya*. Therefore, in order to invoke the deity's pledge, one first calls his name. The actual invocation is thus saying, "Guard my sacred commitments!"

Then as before, the mantra continues with VAJRA SATTVA. For TVENA,[32] first change the body of YUSTAR *yusṭar*. Then put RWATRALA *rwatrala*[33] into the third case of TA *ṭa* to make TVENA.[34] This means "by you,"[35] making "Vajrasattva you." *Uptiṣṭha* ends in the fifth case, so it means "be present!"[36] It is Vajrasattva who is present. When combined with the previous *na*, the mantra reads TVENOPA TISHTHA *tvenopatiṣṭha*.

Vajrasattva is present in oneself, in a firm[37] manner. Therefore, DRIDHO *dṛḍha* is given the SU *sū*[38] of the nominal case, rendering DRIDHO *dṛḍhaḥ*. ME[39] means "for me," as it ends in the dative case marker. Combining these two, DRIDHO MEBHAVA *dṛḍhomebhava* is ending in the fifth,[40] meaning the imperative for the verb "to be." When taken with the previous words, it means, "You, Vajrasattva, be firmly[41] present for me."[42]

Here, the mind without beginning or end is to be understood. As the scriptures state,

---

30 It is in fact vocative.

31 In Sanskrit grammar, SANDHI refers to the various phonological processes that occur at morpheme, or word boundaries.

32 Text reads TVENOPA; however, it only deals with TVENA.

33 It's not possible to guess what YUSTAR *yusṭar* and RWATRALA *rwatrala* may be referring to.

34 Text reads PA, but this does not make sense.

35 Text reads khyod kyi, meaning "your." It should likely read kyod kyis.

36 This is actually a past passive participle in the vocative case.

37 Text reads *brten* or "support."

38 Text reads SU.

39 Text reads KHE.

40 This is not the fifth case but a straight up second-person imperative singular.

41 Text reads *bstren*.

42 Here, two lines have been reduced to one, conflating imperative and vocatives. A literal translation based on my own understanding of the Sanskrit would read "You, present as Vajrasattva, be firm for me!"

Vajrasattva of great joy,
Complete as the essence of Samantabhadra.

This passage explains the ultimate Vajrasattva, in the sense of the abiding nature of things. Here *to be present* means that although he himself pervades and is present in all the animate and inanimate worlds of saṃsāra and nirvāṇa, one has not previously recognized this. Now, may he be present as directly manifest in the manner of one's own self-awareness.

The *yi*[43] prefix is added to TOSHYO *toṣyaḥ*,[44] making SUTOSHYO *sutoṣyaḥ*,[45] which means to be well-satisfied[46] or to be greatly satisfied. *Me* means "for me" and *bhava* is the imperative for "to be." The *visarga* changes to *o*,[47] and when joined, forms SUTOSHYO MEBHAVA *sutoṣyomebhava*. Therefore, one makes an invocation by saying, "Satisfy me greatly with the taste of joy and great bliss, free from change and elaborations."

The invocation is not limited to merely that. Similarly, SUPOSHYO *supoṣyo*[48] means "to expand greatly or excellently." Formulating it with MEBHAVA as above, SUPOSHYO MEBHAVA *supoṣyomebhava*, therefore, means "to expand or nourish me greatly." Giving the SI prefix to RAKTA, it becomes ANU RAKTA *anuraktaḥ*, which means "to be passionate." Adding MEBHAVA makes ANU RAKTA MEBHAVA, which means "Be passionate for me." In actuality, Vajradhara is the name given to the deep compassion of coalescence, which has completely abandoned even the slightest stains of passion or attachment. The mantra is thus saying, "May you embrace me with love."

SARVA means "all" and SIDDHI means "attainment in spiritual practice." Adding the *aṃ* of the accusative case, it becomes SARVA SIDDHI *sarvasiddhiṃ*. ME means "for me." Adding the prefix PRA to YACCHA renders the imperative, "give completely." Therefore, the meaning is, "Complete-

---

43 It seems the author is referring to a special list of names from prefixes; however, I am unfamiliar with them.
44 Text reads TOSYO *toṣyo*.
45 Text reads TOSYAH *toṣyaḥ*.
46 Text reads *len par tshim pa*, however it appears to be a scribal error, as the Sanskrit SU should be translated as *legs*.
47 Text reads U.
48 Text reads SUPOSYOH *supoṣyoḥ*.

ly bestow all attainment upon me." Here *all* refers to all common, extraordinary, coarse, and fine attainments of spiritual practice.

The mantra continues with SARVA, meaning "all," and KARMA, meaning "action." Adding the SU[49] of the locative plural, the word becomes KARMASU. CA is a conjunction meaning "without limit." It is also said[50] to have the meaning of the particle "also." Putting MAR[51] into the genitive case, it means "my." CITTA is put in the accusative by adding an AM *aṃ* and becomes CITTAM *cittaṃ*, which means "mind." SHRE YAM *Śrīyaḥ* means "virtue" and KURU means "to make" in the imperative. Formulating these together, the meaning is "Make my mind virtuous in all actions." This is therefore an invocation that one's mind be made virtuous, because it is the mind that always comes before all activities and because all virtue originates from a virtuous mind. According to the definitive meaning, as the scriptures explain,

> Wherever there is only great bliss,
> The dance of multiplicity is done in the expression of singularity.

The singular vajra of the mind of great bliss manifests a multiplicity of constructs in saṃsara and nirvāṇa, the relative and the ultimate—yet whatever is manifest is never beyond the nature of great bliss. These words are therefore invoking this definitive secret.

HUM is Vajrasattva's seed syllable, which seals the thathāgatas of the five families and signifies the pure nature of the five aggregates. HAHA-HAHAHOH signifies the pure nature of the object of the eyes, such as form and so on, along with the subject of the eyes themselves and the other six consciousnesses. Once perfected, these are all lord thathāgatas.

BHAGAVAN means "lord," or "the one endowed with the four destructions and six fortunes." In order to avoid confusions with the names of the major non-Buddhist gods, the Tibetan translators added the extra syllable *'das*, which means "beyond." SARVA means "all" and TATHAGATA ME MUNCA BHAVA *thathāgata* means "thus-gone one" or "one who has

---

49 Text reads SA SU.
50 Text reads *don med*, which contracts the translated provided below.
51 This should probably read ASMAD.

gone precisely in the manner of ultimate reality or suchness." VAJRA refers to nondual primordial wisdom, and here it is placed in the vocative case.[52] This is to evoke the pledge of all tathāgatas. Altogether, this section can be translated, "O, all lord vajra tathāgatas!"[53]

What is the purpose of invoking the deity's pledge? From MAME MUNCA *māmemuñca, mā* MA is the negative particle for an imperative verb meaning "don't." ME means "for me," and MUNCA is the imperative form of "to abandon." Altogether, this means, "Don't abandon me." Thus in saying, "Make me inseparable from the great bliss of primordial wisdom that realizes suchness," one adds "and never release the grip of deep compassion without reference."

The mantra continues with VAJRI BHAVA. VAJRI means "holding the vajra," and BHAVA is the imperative for "to be." Thus, it means, "Be the vajra holder." This is a clarification of the previous phrase, which supplicates by saying, "Do not release me." Here the manner in which one is not released is being clarified.

MAHA means "great" and SAMAYA refers to the sacred commitments. SATTVA means "being," thus making "Great commitment-being." This means the great being who never transgresses the great time without time. The vocative SI is added to this root, the intention of which is an invocation expressed by AH. This is the indestructible syllable that has the essence of the vajra, along with the speech of all the tathāgatas. Like OM, it exists as embodying all tathāgatas. In this context, it means "without exclusion," or "May I accomplish the essence of the great primordial wisdom that is of equal taste with all of the tathāgatas without exception." Understand it to be invoking this meaning.

The recitation of the mantra purifies the concepts of samsaric names, words, and letters as well as attachment to speech. It arranges the circumstances for the result of enlightened speech to be perfected in the dhātu of the indestructible nāda, so that the wheel of dharma is turned for those to be tamed. And it lays the ground for the purification of prāṇa during the completion stage.

---

52 The text literally reads, "Is attached to the vocative in the first case;" however, the vocative is different from the first or nominal case in Sanskrit grammar.

53 The Sanskrit has Tathāgata in the singular, so it is more likely to mean, "O Lord, Vajra [of all] the Tathāgatas."

As for the benefits of reciting the Hundred Syllables, the root treasure text says,

> By merely reciting this a single time,
> The five actions with immediate results and obscurations are purified.
> Even the place of Narak is emptied
> And you will be inseparable from Vajrasattva.

The Vajra Peak states,

> Even though the five acts of immediate retribution have been committed,
> You will become like Vajrasattva.
> All mudras will be accomplished.
> Everything will be accomplished; there is no doubt.

Thus, understand that it has inconceivable benefits.

III. The Concluding Stages

C. Enlightened Mind, the Suchness of the Completion Stage

The completion stage, based on the development stage, comes when concluding the sessions. It starts with chanting *Appearance and existence melt into light* . . . up until . . . *Again I emerge in the form of Vajrasattva.* The entire vessel and contents, which are pure as the deity, dissolve into the protection circle, which then dissolves into the celestial palace. That dissolves into yourself, the samaysattva Vajrasattva, which then dissolves into the jñānasattva, the moon. That dissolves into the vajra, the vajra into the mantra garland, and the mantra garland into HUNG. HUNG dissolves completely from bottom up into reference-free basic space. There, looking into your natural state, rest in equipoise in that immediate naked state, devoid of any identifiable appearance or awareness. From within that state, arise as the deity for the breaks between sessions, make dedications and aspirations, and enter into your activities.

Regarding the completion stage, it is said,

To be free of the extremes of permanence and nihilism,
Dissolve the mandala gradually into the heart.
Within the reference-free state, arise as the chief figure.
This demonstrates the development and completion stages.

At the final moment of conditioned existence, death or destruction occurs before rising again.
The stages of serially dissolving the pure celestial environment, its inhabitants, the protection enclosure, and the celestial palace into Vajrasattva relates to the [outer elements] dissolving into awareness [at death]. The gradual dissolution of the triple-stacked deity into HUNG relates to the three skies [the appearances of the sky filled with moonlight, the sky filled with rays of sunlight at dawn, and the sky at midnight on the night of a new moon. These are the inner appearances of the dissolution of the inner elements that act as support for conceptual thought]. [Finally, the HUNG] dissolves [from bottom to top] and one experiences luminosity. Having been born in samsara, one is bound to die. Thereafter, as the result of purification [through this Mahāyoga method], the bardo being arises as the form kāya. This is made possible through the mutually dependent arrangements of gathering the suchness kāya into the dhātu and repeatedly arising from this. It is important to practice the completion phase yoga, to keep it fresh, as this lays the foundation for the arising of the kāya of union.

The great tertön had previously taught the completion phase in great detail.

• • •

When Terchen Rinpoche (Chokgyur Lingpa) gave detailed and extensive empowerments and instructions on Vajrasattva and Samyak Heruka of the Secret Heart Essence *to Drubwang Rigdzin Chögyal Dorje, I received them in full. I received them again when the empowerments and instructions of the New Treasures were given to Ngawang Drakpa Gyatso, the fifth supreme Jedrung of Taklung Martang (the Lower Valley). I made notes of the instructions that were given, but for a while did no more than that. Then in the Rat year, when I went to the retreat place Jamling and commenced the recitation, I found that my notes were far too concise and not very clear. Not understanding the stages of meditation, I left the retreat and requested the precious treasure revealer, Lord of the Dharma (Chokgyur Lingpa) for instructions and clarification. Then, with his permission, I committed the instructions to writing. I then adorned them with some additional details from the teachings of the Omniscient Lords of Dharma, the Minling father and son (i.e., Lochen and Terdag Lingpa). Thus, through the kindness of the refuge object in these degenerate times, the great treasure revealer, Guru Vajradhara, these concise instructions that clarify and expand upon the visualization stages for simple, essential practice were written down directly and free of doubt by one who engages in study, reflection, and meditation, the Vinaya holder Pema Drimé Lodrö Shyenpen Chökyi Nangwa during breaks between sessions. May virtue and excellence increase! Virtue!*

Practicing in an Absolute Way

Tulku Urgyen Rinpoche

It is said that the essence of all deities is Vajrasattva, and that the principle of Vajrasattva encompasses the infinite number of peaceful and wrathful buddhas. It is like the analogy of a single moon in the sky that can be reflected simultaneously upon a hundred thousand surfaces of water. All the reflections appear from the same basis of emanation. When the different (pools) of water vanish from the different vessels, the reflection isn't left behind—it is reabsorbed by its source. It doesn't remain anywhere else. In the same way, all the other deities, when dissolved, are absorbed back into the principle of Vajrasattva.

The relationship between the emanations, the buddhas, and the source, or basis, of emanation is like this: From dharmakaya, sambhogakaya manifests; sambhogakaya manifests the five buddha families and also displays the countless, unending forms of peaceful and wrathful deities. There are all different kinds—there is no fixed amount, but an untold number of different ways in which the buddhas manifest. Why is that? It is solely to be able to help sentient beings, who fail to recognize their own nature and who continuously stray into samsaric existence. Out of skillful means, the buddhas and bodhisattvas appear in whatever appropriate (form) is needed in order to influence the deluded sentient beings. We should never think that the buddhas and bodhisattvas are restless and therefore need to go out for a hike, moving around a bit and manifesting all different forms for their own pleasure and entertainment. The state of enlightenment means all personal aims have been totally accomplished. There is nothing more to achieve or attain and so any activity is solely for the welfare of others.

It is not that a particular incarnation of a buddha or bodhisattva appears in the world, for his or her own sake, to carry out one remaining task which he or she had left undone. It is never like that; all personal aims have been completely accomplished. The only activity that buddhas and bodhisattvas engage in is for the sake of others. There is no selfish aim left at all. Therefore, the countless emanations and re-emanations and so forth are all the display of skillful means for the benefit of others.

The basis for emanation is dharmakaya. The emanations themselves are sambhogakaya or nirmanakaya. Normal people cannot perceive the sambhogakaya emanations, which are made of rainbow light. On the other hand, the nirmanakaya is called the "vajra body," comprised of the six elements—in other words, a material body that can be encountered by anyone, regardless of whether that person has pure or impure perception. For example, when Buddha Shakyamuni appeared in this world, pigs and dogs and so forth could also see him. He was not like a sambhogakaya form that can be seen only by high-level bodhisattvas.

The dharmakaya state is our own essence, but we consider the dharmakaya buddha, Samantabhadra, as being "up there" and descending "down here" to give teachings. However, the nature of our own mind, our buddha nature itself, is the dharmakaya buddha. Because we fail to acknowledge this fact, the dharmakaya has to manifest some visible, versatile forms for us to be able to understand what our own nature actually is. [Rinpoche jokingly says, "Actually, the dharmakaya buddha, Samantabhadra, manifests as the sambhogakaya because those to whom the sambhogakaya buddha appears do not recognize that the dharmakaya is their own nature. Therefore, the dharmakaya (assumes) a form that (demonstrates for) us, 'Look here! This is what your nature really is,' and then it explains how the buddha nature is."]

When the buddha nature that is present in everyone appears as a blue buddha outside of ourselves, then our buddha nature is called Samantabhadra, or the dharmakaya buddha. But when it is (left as it is) simply present in everyone, it is called buddha nature.

Sadhana is not something we make up. There is actually no real difference between our buddha nature and the state of dharmakaya of all the buddhas so, rather than this practice being a way of creating an imitation of the state of a buddha, we don't have to create anything. We should allow our nature to be what it actually is, which is no different from that of all the buddhas. Just read the sadhana's lines while leaving the mind in its natural state, and the three samadhis naturally occur.

Why do we need to create the three kayas? They are naturally present. Vajrasattva is the vast base—meaning the dharmakaya—our buddha nature, which is the samadhi of suchness. The *Sangtik Dorsem* sadhana says, *Great bliss, luminosity, is the play of compassion.*[8] That's the example for the sambhogakaya state, which is the second of the three samadhis, the samadhi of illumination. From the display of Samantabhadra, the deity, Vajrasattva, appears. Vajrasattva is holding a vajra and bell to show that appearance and emptiness are indivisible. We cannot separate the two; that's the nirmanakaya level. The whole idea is that the buddhas manifest in all different ways in order to show us what we actually are, our own nature.

First, we should understand the basic idea. Attaining the state of enlightenment simply means becoming (one with) our nature, the dharmakaya state. At that point, all personal aims are achieved; there is nothing more to attain or gain. All the buddhas and bodhisattvas who attained enlightenment have done just that. Having become the state of dharmakaya, they can manifest outwardly as the subtle sambhogakaya forms, which are just like rainbow light, and as the more material nirmanakaya forms. (Both form kayas) appear in many different ways in order to influence and benefit sentient beings. (This activity) occurs only for the sake of others. Understand these two principles: the emanation basis, which is dharmakaya, and the emanation, which is sambhogakaya and nirmanakaya.

All the different forms that are taken, such as different gurus, yidams, dakinis, dakas, dharma protectors, wealth gods, treasure lords, and so forth are all displays of Samantabhadra, the dharmakaya state, which appears in different ways for the benefit of beings. It's not like someone who refreshes himself by moving around. We should acknowledge and appreciate this immense kindness. Actually, whatever we encounter, in terms of the various forms and ways in which the state of buddhahood is manifested, is a great kindness toward us, as the perceiver, because we are deluded and do not recognize our own nature. It is all simply for our own benefit. So, we should acknowledge and appreciate this kindness.

When we engage in the practice of dharma, engaging in virtue and avoiding nonvirtue, it is said that we can achieve enlightenment. The whole reason for saying this is because we have the potential, our nature is potentially the state of enlightenment. A gold lodestone has the potential to yield gold when it is smelted, but a piece of wood does not have this potential, because it doesn't have the nature of gold. However, we do have the (above-mentioned) capacity, because our nature is the enlightened essence. To awaken us to this fact, the state of dharmakaya, or buddhahood, appears in different forms to help us recognize (our own nature). The state of enlightenment appears in an inconceivable (variety of) different forms to influence beings. We should acknowledge that anything that appears before us in our field of experience—whether it is a spiritual friend, an image (or whatever)—and turns our mind toward recognizing our own nature, is, in fact, an emanation of the dharmakaya buddha. It is (showing us) tremendous kindness.

Practice the state of naturalness as you go along; just rest the mind in the natural state while reciting. You don't have to think of anything (at that time.) After you finish bringing to mind the description written here, then continue to chant the mantra, but without thinking of anything during the recitation. There is no real focal point required. If you can't remember the (hundred) syllables of the long mantra, the short six-syllable mantra should be easy to recall. You can chant either mantra without keeping (a focus) in mind; then let your vocal chords do the work. After some time, you will not need to think about moving your fingers on the rosary beads. The mind can just remain in unfabricated naturalness. It will be automatic.

Additional Ways to Practice Vajrasattva

Vajrasattva

The Visualization and Recitation of Vajrasattva

Chokgyur Lingpa

First visualize the deity, the "power of support."

Ah:
Dag gi chiwor peydey teng:
Sangye kün-gyi yeshe ku:
Dorje sempa dewachey:
Drimey tönkey dawey dang:

AH:
Above my head, on a lotus and moon,:
Is the wisdom form of all the buddhas,:
Vajrasattva of great bliss,:
Stainless like the glow of the autumn moon.:

Chagnyi dorje drilbu nam:
Rang ö nyemma gyepar tril:
Dardang rinchen gyen-gyi dzey:
Zhabsung dorje kyiltrung gi:
Jaser tigley longna zhug:

His two hands, holding vajra and bell,:
Joyfully embrace Atopa, his own light.:
Adorned with silks and jewel ornaments,:
And with his two legs in vajra posture,:
He sits in a sphere of bindus and rainbow light.:

Powerful Transformation

While visualizing in this way, and with the "power of remorse"—the intense feeling of regret and sorrow for all evil deeds and failings—practice the antidote, which is the "power of application," the visualization for reciting the mantra.

Tugkar dawey kyilkhor ü:
Desheg kün-gyi tugsog hung:
Yigey gyapey ngagkyi kor:
Depey ötrö dönnyi jey:
Tsurdü dütsi chugyün bab:
Rangi tsangpey goney zhug:
Digdrib nyamchag künjang ney:
Dagching drima meypar gyur:

In the center of the moon disc in his heart,:
Is HUNG, the heart-life of all the sugatas,:
Encircled by the Hundred Syllable mantra.:
By chanting, light shines forth fulfilling the two goals.:
Upon its return, a stream of nectar flows down,:
Entering through the crown of my head,:
It purifies evil deeds, obscurations, and damaged and broken vows,:
Making me pure and immaculate.:

Visualizing this one-pointedly, recite the Hundred Syllable mantra:

OM VAJRA SATTVA SAMAYA: MANU PALAYA: VAJRA SATTVA TVENOPA: TISHTHA DRIDHO MEBHAVA: SUTOSHYO MEBHAVA: SUPOSHYO MEBHAVA: ANU RAKTO MEBHAVA: SARVA SIDDHI ME PRAYACCHA: SARVA KARMA SUCHAME: CHITTAM SHRE YAM: KURU HUNG: HA HA HA HA HOH: BHAGAVAN: SARVA TATHAGATA: VAJRA MAME MUNCA: VAJRI BHAVA: MAHA SAMAYA SATTVA AH:

*Recite this, as well as the quintessence mantra (*OM BENZA SATO AH *or* OM VAJRA SATTVA AH*) as many times as you can. In the end, chant the* Lamenting Apology of Rudra, *or say the following, whichever is suitable:*

Powerful Transformation

Gönpo dagni mishey mongpa yi:
Damtsig leyni galshing nyam:
Lama gönpö kyabdzö chig:
Tsowo dorje dzinpa ni:
Tugje chenpö dagnyi chen:
Drowey tsola dagkyab chi:

Protector, due to my ignorance and delusion,:
I have gone against and broken the samayas.:
Guru, protector, please grant me refuge.:
Supreme vajra-holder,:
With the nature of great compassion,:
To you, the leader of beings, I go for refuge.:

Then say:

Kusung tug tsawa dang yanlag gi damtsig nyamchag tamchey tölshing shagso. Digdrib nyetung drimey tsog tamchey jangshing dagpar dseydu sol

I openly admit all damaged and broken samayas, both the root and branch samayas of body, speech, and mind. Please cleanse and purify all the negative actions, obscurations, failings, and stains I have gathered.

Shey solwa tabpey lama dorje sempa gyeshing dzumpa dang cheypey rigkyi bu khyenam kyi digdrib dagpa yinno shey nangwa jinney rangla timpey gyü jingyi labpar gyur

Guru Vajrasattva is delighted by this prayer, and with a smiling face he says, "Child of noble family, all your negative actions, obscurations, and failings are purified." Thus, he absolves and melts into me, blessing my nature.

Vajrasattva Preliminaries

Tulku Urgyen Rinpoche

We take refuge because, when we look at ourselves, we don't have the omniscient knowledge, the great compassion, or the capacity to benefit others. So we make a request for help to those who possess those qualities of wisdom, compassion, and capacity. This is the same in any mundane task; if we lack the expertise to accomplish something, we turn to those who have the right skills. The Three Jewels do have the capacity to benefit us, in this life, in the following life, and in between—the bardo.

For how long should we take refuge in the Three Jewels? We should take refuge until we, ourselves, become the Three Jewels—when all our obscurations are purified and we have developed the enlightened qualities, then we become the owner of the family of the Three Jewels: We become the Buddha, the Dharma, and the Sangha, and we need not take refuge in anyone else.

Even if we attain the level of an arhat, we will, at some point, have to ask for help or take refuge in those on the bodhisattva bhumis. Even when we attain the bodhisattva levels, we still need to take refuge in the Buddha. But once we become the Buddha, then we are "home," so to speak. We need not take refuge in anyone else because we are "home." So, the basic guideline is that if we lack the power and ability, we put our trust in those who have them.

We arouse bodhichitta because we are all related. All sentient beings have been our own parents. We have a real reason for feeling compassion for them, because they are like our own relatives. This compassion is exactly why buddhas act for the welfare of beings. They have already achieved what they need to achieve for themselves; they don't need anything more than that. Day and night, all buddhas simply watch out for the well-being of others, not for themselves. If after attaining enlightenment one is not concerned with the welfare of others, then one is a despicable buddha. So, for sure we need the bodhichitta attitude.

If we take refuge to free just ourselves from rebirth in the lower realms, which are terrifying, or because we want to free only ourselves from the whole of samsara, then this is a Hinayana attitude of taking refuge. If we take refuge in order to benefit all sentient beings, to lift all of them out of samsara, as well as the passive state of nirvana, and to establish them in enlightenment, then this is the Mahayana attitude, which is called "bodhichitta."

When we engage in the meditation and recitation of Vajrasattva, we have then entered the actual practice of Vajrayana. In this way, the preliminary practices include Hinayana, Mahayana, and Vajrayana.

Vajrasattva is a Sanskrit word—*vajra* signifies "emptiness," while *sattva* signifies "compassion." Therefore, Vajrasattva is the deity that expresses the unity of emptiness and compassion. The word *vajra* means "emptiness" because emptiness is endowed with the seven indestructible, vajra-like qualities: uncuttable, indestructible, firm, solid, true, undefeatable, and unobstructive. Emptiness, like space, is endowed with these seven vajra qualities, and that's why the vajra is used as a synonym for emptiness.

The very fact that the nature of our mind cannot be buried under the earth, flushed away with water, burned by fire, scattered by wind, and so forth means it is totally indestructible. For this reason, it is said that the nature of mind is emptiness.

Sattva means a "compassionate attitude." Compassionate emptiness is the root of all enlightened deities, but, at the same time, compassionate emptiness is also the very foundation of all of samsara and nirvana. Here, the practice is called the meditation and recitation of Vajrasattva. *Meditation* here means what we imagine when we visualize, such as the deity above the crown of our own head, while *recitation* means to chant the mantra.

The Visualization

When practicing Vajrasattva, we don't imagine ourselves in the form of a deity, but as we ordinarily appear. We should think that one cubit distance above the crown of our head, upon a white lotus and moon disc, sits Vajrasattva in actuality, as though in person. He is radiant and effulgent, like a snow mountain reflecting the light of one hundred thousand suns. Feel assured that he is endowed with all the ornaments and attire of a sambhogakaya deity, exactly as they are.

Imagine that within his heart-center is a five-pronged vajra. The central sphere of the vajra should be perfectly round (with a hollow core). A white letter HUNG stands in the center, surrounded by the Hundred Syllable mantra, which coils like a snake around the seed-syllable HUNG in the center.

The Four Remedial Powers

Vajrasattva practice is structured around four remedial powers. The first power is to imagine Vajrasattva, himself, and this is called the "power of the support." The second power is the "power of remorse," whereby you regret negative actions. The third power is the "power of the applied antidote," whereby we imagine that the Hundred Syllable mantra in the center of his heart begins to radiate light that fills his body and exits through his forehead, between his eyebrows. This beam of light shines in all directions and first makes offerings to all buddhas and bodhisattvas in all ten directions, gathering back their blessings and powers. It then sends the light out to all realms of sentient beings, purifying their negative karma and obscurations. That is called "upwardly making offerings and downwardly purifying." The fourth power is the "power of resolve," to vow not to repeat negative actions.

So the first descriptive lines we say begin with the following:

Above my head, on a lotus and moon,[8]

And they end with the following:

He sits in a sphere of bindus and rainbow light.[8]

This visualization is called the "power of the support," whereby we imagine what the lines refer to as we are chanting them.

In short, just visualize the lotus above your head. In other traditions, one must imagine the stem of the lotus rooted in the crown of one's head, but in our tradition we need not do that. Later on, when the text explains how the nectar pours down, in our tradition, it leaves Vajrasattva's right toe and enters us through the crown of our head. In the Nedek tradition, the nectar exits from the toe then enters inside the lotus and makes its way through the stem and finally into the head. You can skip this minor detail.

Vajrasattva combines all buddhas into a single form; therefore, he is called the *wisdom form of all the buddhas*. They are all combined into a single embodiment here. *Vajrasattva of great bliss* means he represents emptiness endowed with the most supreme aspect. That's why even the word *suffering* does not exist in this state of emptiness. The complete absence of suffering must be called "bliss." Therefore, he's "Vajrasattva of great bliss" and not "Vajrasattva of great misery."

He is *stainless like the glow of an autumn moon*. The autumn moon is used as our example, because after the monsoon rains, the dust has been completely washed away from space. Therefore, the moon in autumn is stainless, very clear, and bright. *His two hands, holding vajra and bell* represent skillful means and wisdom: the vajra symbolizes skillful means, or upaya, while the bell symbolizes wisdom, or prajna. He *joyfully embraces Atopa, his own light*. She is his consort, which is actually his own radiation, his own light. He is "beautified" with the adornments of silks and jewels—actually, the thirteen (sambhogakaya) adornments include five silken and eight jeweled ornaments. His legs are in vajra posture and *he sits in a sphere of bindus (little dots of light) and rainbow light*. Visualize him in this way.

After having visualized the "power of support," you practice the second of the four powers, called the "power of remorse," whereby you regret all your former misdeeds and downfalls.

The third is the "power of the applied antidote" and this refers to the visualization of nectar pouring down from Vajrasattva and entering your own system. How should we practice this third power? We visualize a white five-spoked vajra within Vajrasattva's heart center. Within the hollow central sphere of the vajra, which is like a round ball, we visualize a moon disc. Upon this disc is the seed-syllable HUNG, which is the life essence of all the buddhas, or sugatas. This white HUNG is surrounded by the Hundred Syllable mantra-garland, which is written in a counter-clockwise fashion, from left to right, but it turns clockwise. Coiled around the white syllable HUNG like a snake, the "tail of the snake" points a little bit in, while the "head of the snake" points a little bit out. While we recite the Hundred Syllables, this mantra-garland spins clockwise, sending out rays of light fulfilling the two goals: Thus, light radiates out to the infinite buddhafields and presents offerings to infinite buddhas; the light gathers back blessings and again radiates out and purifies the obscurations of all sentient beings.

Recitation and Flow of Nectar

While chanting the mantra, imagine that the mantra-chain starts coiling around the central syllable HUNG and light radiates upward to all the buddhafields, presenting infinite offerings to the countless buddhas. Then the blessings of all the buddhas gather back into you, (in the form of light rays). Again, the light radiates out from the HUNG and its mantra-garland and strikes all sentient beings, purifying their obscurations. Just think this.

When the light returns, a stream of nectar starts flowing from the HUNG with its mantra-garland and completely fills Vajrasattva's body. The nectar then (overflows) and enters through the crown of your head.

Visualize that Vajrasattva and his consort are completely filled with nectar, so that from Vajrasattva's right toe, the nectar overflows and enters you through the crown-chakra and passes down, filling your body. Illnesses, evil influences, karmic misdeeds, broken vows, obscurations, and so forth are forced out of your body and leave through the soles of your feet in the form of all different kinds of disgusting things—pus, rotten blood, small nasty creatures, poisonous insects, and so forth. It all enters the ground, which has opened up beneath us to a depth of seventeen stories. At the bottom, guess who's waiting?—all our karmic creditors, to whom we owe debts such as life, wealth, favors, and so forth. They all appear like the retinue of the Lord of Death, Yama; they are standing there, looking upward and waiting with gapping mouths. All these nasty things enter them and fill their bellies. We should imagine that, through this, all our karmic debts are totally cleared away. At the same time, all these beings, to whom we owe something, are satisfied—and they also develop bodhichitta due to this activity.

At the end, imagine that your body has become totally *pure and immaculate,* like a crystal vase filled with pure milk. So the third power, that of the "applied antidote," is like washing with a very powerful cleansing agent, so not a trace of dirt remains anywhere.

The fourth power is the "power of the resolve," which means that we sincerely vow to ourselves that, "From now on, even at the cost of my life, I will never commit any negative action again." This fourth power is extremely important, because this is what really ensures that negative karma and obscurations are perpetually purified. Otherwise, if we think, "Oh, now I know the trick! I can just purify every negative action as I go along—I can do a little misdeed and then go home and purify! Wow! I've got it made; there's nothing to be afraid of again!" This kind of attitude means we lack the fourth power of resolve, so there is no way to purify anything.

The "power of resolve" is indispensable. If we practice only three of the powers, our practice is incomplete. In order to totally purify misdeeds and obscurations, we must practice in a way in which all four powers are complete. Otherwise, negative propensities will eventually well up again.

As the buddhas have taught, the person who, filled with remorse for misdeeds and obscurations, practices Vajrasattva's meditation and recitation with the four complete remedial powers, will be totally purified, even though his or her evil deeds and obscurations may be as immense as Mount Sumeru. This occurs in the same way that a heap of straw, as high as the tallest mountain in the world, incinerates when a single lit match touches just its corner.

It is said that negative karma and misdeeds have only one good quality—they can be purified through this kind of practice. If misdeeds could not be purified, everything would be hopeless; however, they do have this one good quality. We can eliminate them through Vajrasattva's meditation and recitation.

Once again, these four remedial powers are:

Powerful Transformation

—The power of the support, visualizing Vajrasattva;
—The power of remorse, feeling intense regret for having committed evil, as though you had taken deadly poison;
—The power of the applied antidote, chanting the Hundred Syllable mantra, while imagining the nectar-flow purifying you; and
—The power of resolve, vowing to yourself to never commit evil deeds again, even at the cost of your life.

Apology and Concluding Activities

There is an additional apology chant, called the *Rudra Meshak*. *Meshak* means a "lamenting apology," which is thus chanted with tear-filled eyes. We begin with the feeling, "I am a great sinner. I have really done wrong!" If we do not have the *Rudra Meshak,* which is a long prayer, we can instead chant these six lines:

> Protector, due to my ignorance and delusion,
> I have gone against and broken the samayas.
> Guru, protector, please grant me refuge.
> Supreme vajra-holder,
> With the nature of great compassion,
> To you, leader of beings, I go for refuge.

Protector means Vajrasattva in person. *Supreme vajra-holder* means the "lord of the family," visualized above the crown of your head. Having said these six lines, or the long version, whichever is suitable, then say:

> I openly admit all damaged and broken samayas,
> Both the root and branch samayas of body, speech, and mind.
> Please cleanse and purify all my gathered
> Negative actions, obscurations, failings, and stains!

Praying, thus, Guru Vajrasattva is delighted, and with a smiling countenance, he replies,

Child of noble family, all your negative actions, obscurations, and downfalls are purified.

Thus, we have been absolved. He dissolves into light, which is absorbed into us. In this way, our nature, or stream-of-being is blessed. That is the conclusion of the Vajrasattva practice.

We may wonder, "Where are our negative actions and obscurations found?" Negative karmas and obscurations are not visible, and they are not found in any particular place within the body. However, they are present, lying dormant, in the all-ground, or alaya. What serves as the basis of these latent tendencies of misdeeds and obscurations? The ignorant quality of not knowing our own nature, which is called the "alaya," is "where" the negative karmas find their support. But it is not really a "place." When this alaya is transmuted into awareness wisdom, then negative karmas and obscurations lose their support. There is no longer anywhere for them to stick.

When the old trickster, the ignorant aspect of the alaya, has been chased out—in other words, dissolved—that is the very moment that the great sun of awareness wisdom dawns over the horizon. As this sun rises, the darkness or old "deceiver," who has tricked us for aeons and aeons and aeons, just completely vanishes. The light utterly reveals this deception. This whole deception of samsara is like a sand castle; the nectar of Vajrasattva flushes it away in pieces, and it completely disappears. The falsity of incalculable aeons falls apart, when the alaya is transformed into awareness wisdom. Then everything is wide open, like space—there's no support for samsara. This is called the transformation of the alaya, meaning it becomes awareness wisdom.

This "old trickster" is the deluded mind—the "old deceiver" vanishes without a trace, when awareness wisdom is present. This is what is purified when we use the word buddha, meaning "purified" and "perfected." The "perfected" aspect refers to awareness wisdom, just like the sun that is fully developed as soon as the cloud-formations of dualistic mind have cleared away. Even though the light of awareness wisdom is primordially enlightened or primordially awakened, as soon as the clouds of dualistic mind vanish, we can call it "re-enlightened." Actually, the sun of awareness wisdom is primordially and forever present, as the very identity of the three kayas;

when the clouds and obscurations of deluded mind cover it, it is not visible. When these clouds have been dissolved, it is spontaneously perfected.

In the same way, our deluded thinking has fooled the self-existing wakefulness, which is our nature. Now, the "conman" is falling sick and dying. What will happen next? The good-hearted person is recovering and becoming re-enlightened. So, the trickster of deluded thinking no longer fools awareness wisdom. We are now at the point where the trickster is growing weaker and weaker from sickness, and he is no longer able to work at full power. The sicker he gets, the closer he comes to death. When he finally collapses, awareness wisdom is no longer deceived. This is called "re-enlightenment," which is like the sun shining in the unobscured sky. This was a description of Vajrasattva practice.

Questions and Answers

Question: Can you please explain samayas of body, speech, and mind as well as the root and subsidiary samayas to keep? What do they mean? How should we understand them?'

Rinpoche: Samayas of body, speech, and mind are called "root samayas" and are the main samayas to be observed. They are twofold, as there is an external set and an internal set. The external samayas of body, speech, and mind refer to our relationship with our Vajrayana teacher. We should not harm his body, which is the samaya of the body; we should not violate his command, which is the samaya of speech; and we should not upset his mind, which is the samaya of mind.

Internally, the samaya of body is continually visualizing our body as the yidam deity; the samaya of speech is maintaining the mantra recitation; and the samaya of mind is sustaining our mind in samadhi.

Of course, it is possible to keep the external samayas—we don't beat up our teacher, we don't lie to him, and we don't upset him. If we have not done these things, we have kept the external samaya clean. But the internal samayas are virtually impossible to keep clean—it would mean we are remaining, nonstop, in the state of practice. The moment we become distracted, we have already violated the internal samayas of body, speech, and mind.

Therefore, the moment we have entered Vajrayana, we are, as the well-known example states, like a snake inside a bamboo tube—we can either go up or down, but cannot escape out the sides. Once we have entered into Vajrayana, Vajrasattva practice actually becomes indispensable, because we are constantly violating our samayas.

The four most supreme (ultimate) samayas are called: nonexistence, all-pervasiveness, oneness, and spontaneous perfection. These four require that we remain, nonstop, in the state of awareness wisdom, without any distraction. Of course, we slip away from this, and the moment we slip away, we have already violated our internal Vajrayana samayas. Re-recognizing, again and again, is the most supreme way of mending the violations of samaya. Every day, we should definitely mend our straying from this ultimate samaya by means of Vajrasattva practice. Therefore, it is said that the quintessence of all Vajrayana is the recitation and meditation of Vajrasattva.

Question: Is the visualization done in the same way as the method used during refuge-taking, whereby the image appears instantaneously, or should we build up the visualization of Vajrasattva gradually?

Rinpoche: Do it exactly in the same way, visualizing Vajrasattva in one flash, in an instant. Just think that he is there; that is enough for the visualization. Directly start looking into the visualizer or meditator and try to contact the ultimate Vajrasattva, since he is a representation of your mind's nature.

In Vajrayana, we have the symbol and its meaning. To visualize the iconographical form of Vajrasattva is the symbol, which is your visualization, and to remain in the completion stage, which is the recognition of awareness wisdom is the meaning. Initially, visualize in one flash—pow! he's there—and then go straight to the recognition of mind's nature and, while in that state, recite the mantra.

Question: So the same advice applies—to try to not hold on to the image?

Rinpoche: As I just said, it's completely okay to do the visualization in just one flash and then let go of it and go straight to the mind-nature practice. However, people who are not confident in mind-nature practice and who have a lot of concepts and enjoy attending to a lot of details are, of course, permitted to engage in the solid type of visualization, whereby they build it up gradually, like a house, with first the lotus and then the moon and so forth, going through all the details. But if a person has confidence in his awareness-wisdom practice, it is completely all right to initially visualize Vajrasattva and then go straight to the mind-nature practice. That's fine.

Question: Do we chant the Hundred Syllable mantra aloud or do we say it silently?

Rinpoche: In general, peaceful mantras of peaceful deities are recited so that you, yourself, can hear it, while wrathful mantras are recited under your breath. Don't recite too loudly, don't recite too softly, don't recite too fast, and don't recite too slow—just recite at a normal speed and (modulation.) Don't do the speed recitations that some people get into, and also not like a grandmother talking in her sleep.

Question: Someone told me if we speak even a single ordinary word during our recitation, the whole practice is spoiled.

Rinpoche: Yes, during the time of recitation, you should not interrupt the recitation session with ordinary speech. Tell yourself you won't engage in ordinary conversation until the session is complete. You should not be reciting the mantra, OM VAJRA SATTVA SAMAYA..., while listening with one ear to your neighbors having a conversation, whereby you suddenly say, "Hey, what did you just say?" This interrupts the recitation.

Question: Should we do our visualizations with our eyes open or closed?

Rinpoche: The main focus in this teaching on Dorje Sempa[54] is the practice of rigpa, or awareness. In the practice of awareness, it is said we should always keep our eyes open. Personally, I advise students to keep their eyes open. Why? Because the eyes are said to be the "gates through which wisdom appears." In some practices, wisdom beings appear in front of our eyes. If we keep our eyes closed, we won't see anything. In Dzogchen, the advice is always to keep the eyes wide open. So, in the case of visualization and recitation, keep the eyes open.

Question: If one is so tired that the eyes fall shut so that one falls asleep, after one wakes up should one continue the meditation?

Rinpoche: Whenever your mind is very tired, drowsy, or dull, take off your clothes, open your window, go outside and do some exercises, and freshen your mind. When you feel drowsy, look out into empty space;

---

54 Dorje Sempa is Tibetan, while Vajrasattva is Sanskrit, but the deity is the same.

look out at the sky. When you are agitated and very nervous, relax completely from within. Lower your gaze and focus your mind on the region of your navel. You will become completely relaxed. These techniques are methods to counter drowsiness and agitation.

The two great obstacles to practice are drowsiness and agitation. As our mind has the two aspects of being empty and cognizant, the display of the emptiness aspect is drowsiness and the display of the cognizant aspect is agitation. Even if the thick clouds have vanished and the fog has melted away, there may still be a faint haze obscuring space. Therefore, an obscuration still exists. In the same way, the gross concepts and medium concepts may have been cleared away, but still a veil of subtle concepts can obscure your practice. Even the most subtle meditation experience still occurs within the conceptual obscuration. Only when all obscurations, all meditation experiences, and all the subtle veils are completely gone is the naked awareness wisdom revealed.

Question: Rinpoche, are you saying the qualities of awareness, such as steadiness or a very concentrated samadhi, are also subtle obscurations?

Rinpoche: The one-pointed concentrated mind is a conceptual state. This is definitely an obscuration, (which clouds) awareness. All these different obscurations (clouding) mind-nature can be very, very subtle. For example, even if musk is removed from a container, the container still retains the odor of the musk. Similarly, our habitual tendencies or patterns still linger during our practice and obscure the practice.

Question: In the context of this practice, how many *Rudra Meshak* apology chants should we try to complete?

Rinpoche: When you do a short Vajrasattva session, you only need to say the brief Essential Apology prayer, which begins with, "Protector, due to my ignorance and delusion". Recite this prayer during every Vajrasattva session. If you are very diligent, you can recite the longer prayer, *Rudra Meshak*, once during every session. If you are more lazy, you can recite this longer prayer just once a day in the evening. But it's completely all right just to repeat the short apology with each short session.

The Abridged Daily Practice of Vajrasattva

ADAPTED BY *Kyabje Dilgo Khyentse Rinpoche*

Begin with repeating refuge and bodhichitta three times:

Namo, rigkün kyabdag lama jey:
Ngödrub jungney yidam lha:
Barchey künsel khandro ma:
Tsawa sumla kyabsu chi:

NAMO:
In the lord guru, the sovereign of all buddha families;:
In the yidam deity, the source of accomplishment;:
And in the dakinis, who dispel all obstacles;:
I take refuge in the Three Roots.:

Ho, ma gyur semchen tamchey kün:
Sang gyey gopang tobjey chir:
Nyechö kündom gechö dü:
Shenpen jangsem tagtu kyey:

HOH:
In order that all beings, my mothers,:
May attain the level of buddhahood,:
I will continuously develop the bodhichitta by refraining from all misdeeds,:
Practicing virtuous actions, and benefiting others.:

Second, the main practice:

Ah:
Dorje sempa namkha chey:
Zungwey mizin chuda dra:
Küntu sangpö rölpa ley:
Tabshey zungjug tsawey lha:
Sempa karpo dordril nam:
Rang ö yumkyü detong jor:
Dardang rinchen gyen gyi gyen:
Machö lhugpey ngang nyi ley:
Tsowö tugkar shiwa dang:
Chiwor traktung lhatsog sal:
Tugkar nyidey ga-u ü:
Hung ley ngag kyi trengwey kor:
Özer trodü dön nyi chey:
Nyamchag togdrib yingsu jang:
Nöchü shitro rabjam kyi:
Lha ngag yeshe rölpar shar:

AH:
Vajrasattva is vast space,:
Intangible, as the moon on water.:
From the display of Samantabhadra,:
The root deity, unity of means and knowledge,:
White Vajrasattva, holding vajra and bell,:
Adorned with silk and jewel ornaments,:
Embraces the consort, his own radiance, the union of bliss and emptiness.:

Within this state of uncontrived naturalness,:
In the heart center of the chief figure are the peaceful deities.:
In the crown center the heruka deities manifest.:
In the middle of the sun and moon sphere within the heart center,:
HUNG is encircled by the mantra-garland.:
Rays of light radiate and return, accomplishing the two benefits,:
Spontaneously purifying violations, breaches, and conceptual obscurations.:

Powerful Transformation

The world and beings appear as the display of deities, mantras, and wisdom:
Of the all-encompassing peaceful and wrathful ones.

Thus, recite the Vajrasattva mantra:

Om benza sato ah:
OM VAJRA SATTVA AH:

Thus, recite the general mantra for the peaceful ones:

Om bodhichitta mahasukha gyanadhatu ah:
OM BODHICHITTA MAHA SUKHA JNANA DHATU AH:

Thus, recite the general mantra for the wrathful ones:

Om rulu rulu hung jo hung:
OM RULU RULU HUNG BHYO HUNG:

At the end of the session, say HUNG HUNG HUNG *to dissolve in luminosity. Then say* PHAT PHAT PHAT *to emerge as the deity of the post-meditation.*

Next, seal with dedication and aspiration:

Gewa diyi nyurdu dag:
Dorje sempa drub gyur ney:
Drowa chig kyang malü pa:
Dey yi sala göpar shog:

Through this merit, may I swiftly:
Accomplish Vajrasattva,:
And place every being without exception:
In that very state.:

• • •

This was adapted from the Sheldam Nyingjang of Tukdrub *by Mangala, Kyabje Dilgo Khyentse Rinpoche.*

Commentary on the Abridged Daily Practice of Vajrasattva

Tulku Urgyen Rinpoche

Vajrasattva is the deity who represents the unity of emptiness and compassion. *Vajra* refers to the profound emptiness and *sattva* means compassion. The unity of emptiness and compassion is the buddha nature, also called the unity of emptiness and knowingness or the unity of emptiness and awareness; this is the real Vajrasattva.

Vajrasattva, who encompasses all families, pervades all the five families of victors. Within Vajrasattva, the one hundred families of the Secret Mantrayana are condensed into one. This refers to the hundred peaceful and wrathful deities, who are combined into the single deity, Vajrasattva.

The most supreme practice to purify misdeeds and obscurations is the practice of Vajrasattva. Actually, Vajrasattva is no different from the primordial Buddha Samantabhadra. When Samantabhadra is adorned with ornaments, he is called Vajradhara; Vajradhara again manifests as Vajrasattva. These three buddhas are one in essence.

All schools in Tibet practice Vajrasattva, but there are numerous Vajrasattva practices within those various schools. Some Vajrasattva practices are very extensive and some are brief. This particular Vajrasattva practice is an abridged form for daily practice. In this text, the practices of Mahayoga, Anuyoga, and Atiyoga are condensed into one sadhana. This small sadhana was extracted from the *Tukdrub Sheldam Nyingjang (thugs sgrub zhal gdams snying byang)*, the root tantra of the *Lamay Tukdrub Barchay Kunsel (bla ma'i thugs sgrub bar chad kun sel)* cycle. This cycle is one of the most famous terma-treasures of Chokgyur Dechen Lingpa. Kyabje Dilgo Khyentse Rinpoche extracted this text from the *Sheldam Nying-*

jang, added some lines to it, and arranged it in its present form. Except for these additional lines, the entire text is a terma-treasure of Chokgyur Lingpa.

Our misdeeds, obscurations, and habitual patterns are the primary causes preventing meditation experiences and realization from arising. There are countless purification practices, but among all of them, the recitation and meditation of Vajrasattva is the most supreme. If we truly confess and regret our misdeeds committed in this and countless former lifetimes, it is possible to purify every one of them. Misdeeds have only one quality: They can be purified through confession.

Every Vajrasattva practice requires the four powers: the power of the support, the power of regret, the power of resolution, and the power of the applied antidote.

The power of the support in this sadhana is the visualization of Vajrasattva as the object for confession. But, also a spiritual master, a statue, the buddhist scriptures, or a stupa are suitable as an object for confession and are considered to be the power of the support.

Here, in this sadhana, you begin with refuge and the development of bodhichitta, which is indispensable for confession practice. Even if we have all four powers included in our practice, if we lack bodhichitta, we will not be able to purify misdeeds and obscurations. It is said that when genuine bodhichitta is born within our mind, all former misdeeds are naturally purified.

The power of regret means to develop strong regret for all past misdeeds and nonvirtuous actions. First, we need to be able to recognize our misdeeds as such, and then sincerely and truly confess them with deep felt regret to Vajrasattva.

The power of resolution means to remember all our countless former misdeeds, and to think, "From now on, even at the cost of my life, I will refrain from committing any further misdeeds." Develop a strong and unshakable resolve to abstain from further negative actions.

The power of the antidote is any virtuous activity, such as taking refuge, developing bodhichitta, doing prostrations, rejoicing in the merit of others, dedicating merit, and so forth. In particular, it refers to this practice of Vajrasattva, visualizing oneself as Vajrasattva, reciting the Vajrasattva mantra, and resting in samadhi.

All buddhist practices start with refuge and bodhichitta. As long as we haven't attained complete enlightenment, we need to rely on an object of refuge. Once we attain enlightenment, we, ourselves, become the objects of refuge for others.

To simplify, it is perfectly all right to visualize Vajrasattva and his consort as the objects of refuge. Vajrasattva is like the sun disc, which includes all the rays of light. Within Vajrasattva and consort, all the objects of the ninefold refuge are included. On the outer level, Vajrasattva's body is the Sangha, his speech is the sacred Dharma, and his mind is the Buddha. On the inner level, his body is the guru, his speech is the yidam, and his mind is the dakini. On the secret level, his body is the dharmakaya, his speech is the sambhogakaya, and his mind is the nirmanakaya. Visualize Vajrasattva and consort as the embodiment of the ninefold refuge, sitting in front of you in the middle of space on a lotus with sun and moon discs.

When reciting the lines of refuge three times, visualize the objects of refuge in front, but know that the ultimate refuge is our own buddha nature endowed with the three kayas.

NAMO:
In the lord guru, the sovereign of all buddha families;
In the yidam deity, the source of accomplishment;
And in the dakinis, who dispel all obstacles;
I take refuge in the Three Roots.

The yidam deity is *the source of accomplishments*. Vajrasattva is the yidam deity, which is the source of all accomplishments, relative and supreme. The supreme accomplishment is the attainment of enlightenment, and the relative accomplishments are the eight ordinary siddhis: the sword, the pill, the eye medicine, the swift foot, extracting the essence, travelling to the celestial field, invisibility, and perceiving treasures beneath the earth.

The yidam is the deity with whom you share the single samaya. The root of the yidam deity is self-existing wisdom. To meet the real yidam deity, first recognize self-existing wisdom. The yidam is the root of accomplishments. All the accomplishments come from self-existing awareness. The most essential yidams are the hundred peaceful and wrathful deities. The quintessence of the hundred deities is Vajrasattva. The main point to understand is that the deity is your own mind. To think that the deity is something outside will postpone the attainment of accomplishments. The deity is your own awareness wisdom. When you have truly recognized your mind-essence, you have already met the deity face-to-face. Knowing that, develop the confidence in thinking, "I am the deity." This is actually knowing it for what it is.

The dakini is the remover of all obstacles. The dakini is a female buddha, such as Samantabhadri, the five female buddhas, the eight female bodhisattvas, and so forth. The dakini is the root that *dispels all obstacles*. The dakinis and the dharmapalas comprise the root of activities and this activity is extremely swift.

Dakini, in this sadhana, refers to the consort of Vajrasattva, white Atopa. The real dakini is the expression of your awareness. Vajrasattva and consort symbolize the unity of perception and emptiness.

I take refuge in the Three Roots.[8] The guru, yidam, and dakini are awareness wisdom. The three kayas are awareness wisdom. As awareness wisdom pervades all sentient beings, it permeates their body, speech, and mind. It pervades all of samsara and nirvana. Whoever has a mind, has the buddha nature. Once we have stabilized the recognition of awareness wisdom, we will perceive everything as infinite purity. Within this view, the five great elements are the five female buddhas. The five aggregates are the five male buddhas. Everything that appears is the expression of awareness. Both samsara and nirvana are the expression of awareness; the only difference between samsara and nirvana is whether or not awareness wisdom is recognized. Not having recognized awareness wisdom, we perceive its impure expression arising as samsara. However, having recognized and stabilized awareness wisdom, we will experience its pure expression arising as nirvana.

While maintaining the recognition of awareness, recite the lines of refuge three times. At the end, think that light radiates out from all the objects of refuge and purifies all your misdeeds and obscurations and those of all sentient beings. Think that through this, all misdeeds and obscurations are actually purified. Finally, all refuge objects dissolve into the central figure, Vajrasattva, who in turn melts into light, and the light dissolves into you. This completes the taking of refuge.

Now generate bodhichitta. To generate bodhichitta refers to the relative and the absolute bodhichitta.

Hoн:
In order that all beings, my mothers,
May attain the level of buddhahood,

All sentient beings have been my father and mother in former lifetimes. Bringing to mind that all sentient beings of the three realms of samsara have been our mothers and that they have been circling in samsara since beginningless time, generate compassion. Developing kindness and compassion towards all sentient beings, wishing to establish them in the state of happiness, and ultimately in the state of complete enlightenment, is the practice of bodhichitta.

The attitude of wanting them to be free from suffering, to have happiness, and making the wish, "May they attain the state of complete buddhahood," is the bodhichitta practice.

The level of buddhahood means the state in which there is not even the slightest mention of suffering. It is the path of perfect happiness. The state of buddhahood is devoid of all mistakes and endowed with inconceivable qualities. Buddhahood is the state of the actualized buddha nature. We need to first recognize buddha nature, then train in this recognition, and finally stabilize it.

I will continuously develop the bodhichitta by refraining from all misdeeds,
Practicing virtuous actions, and benefiting others.

Generating compassion and practicing the six perfections, or transcendental actions, is the relative bodhichitta. Recognizing awareness wisdom is the absolute bodhichitta. This is the view, free from observer, observing, and object observed. The view is free from the four extremes, which are existence, nonexistence, both, and neither. In short, the relative bodhichitta is compassion and the absolute bodhichitta is the recognition of buddha nature.

Compassion can be contrived or uncontrived. Contrived compassion means to think about the suffering of all beings and feel sorry for them. Uncontrived compassion arises from the recognition of the buddha nature. If you genuinely recognize buddha nature, you will realize how special and precious it actually is. You directly see that all sentient beings have this perfect buddha nature. But, due to their lack of recognition, they have been tormented by inconceivable sufferings since beginningless time. You will think to yourself, "I have realized it, but they, although they have it, do not realize it." At this moment, a heartfelt, natural compassion will arise in your own mind towards all sentient beings. The more you get accustomed to the recognition of buddha nature, the more natural compassion will arise. Based on this kind of compassion, you naturally want to ease their suffering and guide them to the level of complete enlightenment.

In this sadhana, the lines of bodhichitta include both the relative and the absolute bodhichitta. To develop bodhichitta is the intent of the precious Mahayana teachings. Repeat the lines of bodhichitta three times.

When generating bodhichitta, the visualization is the same as when taking refuge. Now, the buddhas, bodhisattvas, gurus, yidams, dakinis, and dharmapalas are not the objects of refuge but, instead, are the witnesses to your bodhichitta vow. After you have dissolved the visualization of refuge into yourself, visualize the entire refuge assembly once again in front of you for the bodhichitta practice.

Having repeated the lines of bodhichitta three times, train in the giving of happiness and taking of suffering. Imagine transferring all your happiness, health, merit, and riches to all sentient beings. Think that they become perfectly happy and content. In return, imagine that you take upon yourself all of their suffering, bad karma, and troubles. By doing this, you train yourself in the practice of giving and taking. You may combine this giving with breathing out, and taking with breathing in.

At the end of bodhichitta practice, imagine that light goes out from all the buddhas and bodhisattvas to purify all the misdeeds of you and others. After that, the assembly of the buddhas melts into light and that light dissolves into you. Imagine that you and the buddhas have become one. Rest a moment in the nonconceptual state.

The main practice is next. Before even starting with development stage practice, we must first know who the deity is, namely our awareness wisdom. Do not think the deity is something other than that. A quotation from the scriptures states, "I am the deity and the deity is myself." This means that the buddha nature is the deity and the deity is the buddha nature. Before attempting to accomplish the deity, first identify it in this way. Identifying the real deity involves recognizing awareness. Once you have recognized awareness, you will quickly accomplish the yidam deity, while doing the sadhana practice.

Thinking the yidam deity is external is like searching for an elephant outside of the house, without knowing it is already standing inside. Wherever there is buddha nature, there is also the yidam deity. The deity is not our dualistic mind, but the essence of our mind, awareness wisdom. It is the unity of the empty essence and cognizant nature.

The deity itself arises from self-existing awareness, the buddha nature. The buddha nature is endowed with kayas and wisdoms. These are the three kayas and their respective wisdoms. The empty essence is the dharmakaya. This kaya is a space-like body, whose wisdom is the dharmadhatu wisdom. The cognizant aspect is the sambhogakaya. This kaya is a light body, endowed with the five wisdoms of the five families of victors. The unified capacity is the nirmanakaya. This kaya is the vajra body, endowed with the six elements. The nirmanakaya wisdom is the wisdom of knowing the natural state and the wisdom of knowing whatever there is to know. All these kayas and wisdoms are inherent within awareness wisdom.

Awareness wisdom, rigpa, is primordial purity. From the expression of awareness, spontaneous manifestations, the forms of infinite deities manifest. All deities are inherently present within awareness wisdom.

The main practice itself starts with the realization of the three kayas, which corresponds to the three samadhis. The realization of the dharmakaya is the suchness samadhi. This is the emptiness aspect of the mind. The realization of the sambhogakaya is the all-illuminating samadhi. This is the cognizant aspect of the mind. The unity of both the emptiness aspect and the cognizant aspect is the realization of the nirmanakaya, the seed-syllable samadhi.

The visualization develops out of the three kayas.[x] As you are endowed with the buddha nature, you possess the three kayas. They cannot be created or fabricated; you naturally have them. When you recognize your buddha nature, the three kayas are spontaneously present. As they are spontaneously present, you do not need to do anything at all besides recognize your awareness wisdom.

If you can, practice Vajrasattva as unfolding from the state of awareness, rigpa. Within that state, you visualize Vajrasattva in a single instant. The ultimate form of the development stage is called "visualization in a single instant." Visualize all the deities in one flash, like an image reflected in a mirror. Think once, "I am Vajrasattva adorned with all the garments and ornaments." That is enough. From within the expression of awareness, the visualization clearly manifests. Without moving away from the state of primordial purity, the spontaneous manifestations arise in the form of the yidam deity.

When you hold a mirror in front of a thangka, it is reflected within the mirror in a single instant. Or, when you press the button of a flashlight or torch, the light appears instantly. This is like visualization in a single flash. Within the recognition of awareness, you think, "The appearance aspect is the yidam deity." By thinking this within the state of awareness, the unity of both development and completion stages is accomplished. This is the practice of those of highest capacity.

Recognizing awareness is the genuine suchness samadhi. Within that state of recognition, natural compassion develops; that is the all-illuminating samadhi. *Vajra* in Vajrasattva stands for emptiness, the suchness samadhi. *Sattva* means compassion, the all-illuminating samadhi. Vajrasattva himself, being the unity of emptiness and compassion, is the seed-syllable samadhi. There is no need here to develop Vajrasattva out of a seed syllable as in other sadhanas. The manifest form of Vajrasattva, himself, is the seed-syllable samadhi. In other words, as this is an Atiyoga practice, you do not need to first visualize the seed-syllable HUNG, which then turns into Vajrasattva. Here, Vajrasattva manifests directly within awareness.

AH. Vajrasattva is vast space.⁸

The syllable AH is the root of all deities, mantras, and samadhis. It is the sound of the unborn. *Vajra* in Vajrasattva means emptiness and *sattva* means compassion. The unity of emptiness and compassion is the unchanging great bliss, which is devoid of even the slightest mention of suffering. This is the deity Vajrasattva.

The vajra, symbolizing emptiness, is a metaphor for space. The vajra has seven qualities. They are the qualities of being uncuttable, indestructible, true, firm, stable, unobstructable, and unassailable. Emptiness is similar to space, which cannot be destroyed or altered in any way. It cannot be burned by fire or washed away by water. This space and vajra-like emptiness is the suchness samadhi. The space-like dharmakaya is the base from which Vajrasattva emanates.

Vajrasattva is vast space§ indicates the realization of the suchness samadhi, the dharmakaya.

The essence is empty, but its nature is cognizant; compassion arises from the cognizant aspect. Physical space is only empty; it lacks the cognizant aspect. It does not know or feel anything. But, the empty essence of the mind is endowed with the cognizant nature. Its emptiness aspect is similar to space and its cognizant aspect is like the sun within space. The empty mind is knowing and cognizant. The cognizant aspect is called compassion, the all-illuminating samadhi.

Both the buddha nature and the dualistic mind are empty and cognizant. It is one entity with two possibilities. When buddha nature is recognized, it is called the "unity of being empty and cognizant, with the core of awareness." When not recognized, it is then called the "unity of being empty and cognizant, with the core of ignorance or nonawareness."

Intangible, as the moon on water.§

This line indicates the realization of the all-illuminating samadhi, the sambhogakaya. The sambhogakaya is visible but without any solidity. It is like the moon reflected on water. Imagine the form of Vajrasattva as being visible yet intangible, like a rainbow appearing within the sky.

On chanting this line in the sadhana, the deity is manifest. This line also indicates the seed-syllable samadhi. The deity is the unity of the empty essence and the cognizant nature; it is the basis from which all deities manifest. A scripture states,

> The essence abides as body,
> The nature is manifest as speech,
> And the capacity radiates as mind.

The expression of the all-encompassing capacity manifests as the visualization of Vajrasattva. Within awareness, rigpa, all three kayas are naturally complete. The expression of awareness manifests as the deity

Vajrasattva. This awareness expression is utterly unimpeded and unrestricted. Without losing the recognition of awareness, visualize the deity. This capability is called the expression of awareness. From it, the inconceivable qualities of knowing-wisdom, loving-kindness, enabling-activities, and sheltering-powers manifest.

While maintaining the recognition of awareness, one can perform all activities, such as pacifying, enriching, magnetizing, subjugating, and the supreme activity. To visualize Vajrasattva within the state of awareness is called the "unity of both the development and the completion stages". The development stage without completion stage is a conceptual practice. Endeavor to practice both simultaneously.

Conversely, if you have not recognized awareness, you have no choice but to mentally create emptiness. You have to think, "The universe and beings are all empty." Then think, "Within this conceptual emptiness, I manifest the celestial palace, the deity and so forth." You link one positive thought to the next and create a mental replica of the real deity.

Vajrasattva is the unity of perception and emptiness. The two examples for the unity of emptiness and perception are the moon reflected on water and the rainbow within the sky. You can see them, but you cannot take hold of them. Likewise, visualize Vajrasattva to be visible, but without having any concrete physical nature. From the space-like dharmakaya, the emanation appears, like a moon reflected on water. It appears but has no self-nature. These emanations are both the sambhogakaya and the nirmanakaya.

Intangible, as the moon on water, Vajrasattva is visible as an apparent form; but as he is empty in essence, he cannot be grasped. The moment Vajrasattva manifests, the seed-syllable samadhi is accomplished. At that moment, think, "I am Vajrasattva." Generate the confidence that you actually are Vajrasattva; this confidence is called "stable pride."

There are three characteristics of visualization: vivid presence, pure recollection, and stable pride. Vivid presence is to have a sharp and clear image of the deity. Pure recollection is to think of the symbolic meaning of the deities: their form, their consorts, their ornaments, and so forth. One reflects on the symbols, the signs, and the meaning. Stable pride is to generate the confidence that you are the deity. You are completely sure that you are Vajrasattva. Do not entertain doubts like, "Maybe I am Vajrasattva, and maybe not."

Among these three types, stable pride is the most eminent and important. This is the confidence that you are the yidam deity Vajrasattva. The practice of the post-meditation deity is to maintain this confidence, thinking, "I am Vajrasattva," even after your practice session is over.

From the display of Samantabhadra,§

Samantabhadra is the dharmakaya buddha, Vajradhara is the sambhogakaya buddha, and Vajrasattva is the nirmanakaya buddha. Think, "I am Vajrasattva. I am the display of Samantabhadra. My mind and Vajrasattva's mind are inseparable." The meaning of the word *display* here is identical with the word *emanation*. Vajrasattva is the emanation of Samantabhadra, and he is the display of your own awareness.

The root deity, unity of means and knowledge,§

The unity of means and knowledge§ refers to the unity of Vajrasattva and his consort, who is his own manifestation. *Means* also signifies "compassion," and *knowledge* indicates "emptiness." Vajrasattva is the unity of compassion and knowledge. Without the unity of skillful means and knowledge, you cannot attain enlightenment.

In Mahayana, the unity of knowledge and skillful means refers to the unity of emptiness and compassion. In Mahayoga, it refers to the unity of the development stage and the completion stage. In Atiyoga, it refers to the unity of Trekchö and Tögal.

White Vajrasattva, holding vajra and bell,§

Visualize a lotus flower with one thousand petals in full bloom. Sitting upon it is the seat of a full moon. On top of that, visualize yourself as Vajrasattva. His body is white like a massive snow mountain struck by the light of one hundred-thousand suns. He has one face and two hands. In his right hand, he holds the golden five-pronged vajra of empty awareness at the level of his heart center. With his left hand, he supports the white silver bell of empty appearances upon his thigh. His jet black hair, tied up in a top knot, is ornamented with a precious band and a jewel crest.

Adorned with silk and jewel ornaments,⁂

He is adorned with the five silken garments: the silk shawl on the upper part of his body, the leggings of multi-colored silk on the lower part of his body, the silken tiara, the silk ribbons, and the silk jacket. Some commentaries mention a silken girdle instead of the silk jacket.

He also wears the eight jewel ornaments: the jewel crown, right and left earrings, throat ornaments, bracelets, anklets, belt, the long necklace, and the short necklace. Some commentaries list the shoulder ornaments instead of the belt. Also they count the long and short necklace as one and, in addition, list finger rings. This is the thirteenfold sambhogakaya attire.

Embraces the consort, his own radiance, the union of bliss and emptiness.⁂

He embraces his consort, who is his own radiance. Vajrasattva is like a crystal, and Atopa is the rainbow light emitted from that crystal.

Atopa is white, and holding a curved knife and a skull cup, she embraces Vajrasattva. Both of them are dignified by the nine peaceful expressions. With his feet in the vajra posture, he sits as the essence of nondual bliss and emptiness, in a sphere of rainbow lights and circles.

The union of bliss and emptiness⁂ refers to emptiness endowed with the supreme of all aspects, and the unchanging great bliss. As emptiness is devoid of all concepts, it is beyond suffering; it cannot be tainted by even the slightest suffering. It is the utterly unchanging state of buddhahood. That aspect of emptiness is called "great bliss." This bliss is nondual and undefiled.

Vajrasattva and consort also symbolize the primordial unity of perception and emptiness. Vajrasattva represents the perception aspect and his consort Vajratopa represents the emptiness aspect.

Within this state of uncontrived naturalness,⁂

Visualize Vajrasattva in the state of unfabricated naturalness. *Uncontrived* means "unmodified," and *naturalness* means to leave it simply as it is. The state of uncontrived naturalness is the state of awareness wisdom.

Powerful Transformation

In the heart center of the chief figure are the peaceful deities.§

In the heart center of the chief figure, Vajrasattva, are the forty-two peaceful deities. It is said that these peaceful deities abide within the heart center of all sentient beings. It is also said that the buddha nature abides in the heart.

In the crown center, the heruka deities manifest.§

In Vajrasattva's crown center, his skull mansion, are the fifty-eight blood drinking deities, the herukas. The term *heruka* refers to wrathful deities. The *he* in heruka means "enjoying" or "drinking," the *ru* means "blood," and the *ka* means "skull cup" *(kapala)*. In this way, the word *heruka* means the "one who drinks blood from the skull cup." All the peaceful and wrathful deities reside in Vajrasattva's body.

In this practice, the mandala of your own body contains only the peaceful deities in the heart center and the wrathful deities in the crown center. In more extensive practices, the mandala of your own body also contains the assembly of the vidyadhara deities in the throat center, Vajrayogini in the navel center, and Vajrakumara in the secret place. But, it is completely sufficient for this practice to just visualize the peaceful and wrathful deities within your body.

In the middle of the sun and moon sphere within the heart center,§

Imagine that in Vajrasattva's heart center are the forty-two peaceful deities. The central figure of the forty-two peaceful deities is Samantabhadra and his consort Samantabhadri. In Samantabhadra's heart center are the two hemispheres of the sun and moon, joined together. The hemisphere of the sun is below and the hemisphere of the moon is above; together, they form a round ball.

Further imagine that in Vajrasattva's crown center are the fifty-eight wrathful deities. The central figure of the fifty-eight wrathful deities is Chemchok Heruka and his consort Trotishvari. In Chemchok Heruka's heart center, there are also two hemispheres of sun and moon joined together in the same way.

Powerful Transformation

In the middle of the sun and moon sphere within the heart center,⁑
HUNG is encircled by the mantra garland.⁑

Imagine a white or light blue seed-syllable HUNG within the two joined hemispheres of sun and moon within the heart center of Samantabhadra, and a dark blue seed-syllable HUNG within the two joined hemispheres of sun and moon in the heart center of Chemchok Heruka. Around both seed syllables, a mantra garland of the Hundred Syllable mantra of Vajrasattva is coiling like a snake. The color of each mantra garland corresponds to the color of the respective seed syllable. While reciting the long and the short mantra of Vajrasattva, visualize the circling of the Hundred Syllable mantra garlands. Both mantra garlands are coiling simultaneously around their respective seed syllables.

If you do not have sufficient time, recite the short Vajrasattva mantra. If you have sufficient time, first chant one hundred, or a minimum of twenty-one, recitations of the Hundred Syllable mantra. After this, recite the short Vajrasattva mantra as much as you can. In both cases, visualize the mantra garlands of the Hundred Syllable mantra coiling around the two seed syllables in a clockwise fashion.

When you recite the mantra for the peaceful and wrathful deities, you may visualize the white or light blue mantra garland of the peaceful deities, the Bodhichitta mantra, around the HUNG within Samantabhadra's heart center. Simultaneously, imagine the dark blue mantra garland of the wrathful deities, the Rulu Rulu mantra, around the HUNG within Chemchok Heruka's heart center.

Consider the Hundred Syllable mantra of Vajrasattva to be the extensive mantra for the peaceful and wrathful deities. Every syllable of the Hundred Syllable mantra represents one of the hundred peaceful and wrathful deities. The Bodhichitta mantra and the Rulu Rulu mantra are the short mantras for the peaceful and wrathful deities.

Alternatively, you may visualize the Hundred Syllable mantra combined with the Bodhichitta mantra in Samantabhadra's heart and the Hundred Syllable mantra combined with the Rulu Rulu mantra in Chemchok Heruka's heart. In this case, the mantras would be attached one after the other, joined into a long mantra garland.

Actually, each seed-syllable HUNG within the heart centers of Samantabhadra and Chemchok Heruka is like the sun in the sky. For example, wherever there is water in the world, the image of the sun is reflected. One single sun is reflected in many pools. Likewise, it is all right to think that the syllable HUNG and the mantra garland are within the heart centers of each of the peaceful and wrathful deities.

As I said earlier, our misdeeds, obscurations, and habitual patterns are the primary causes preventing our meditation experiences and realization from arising. Now by practicing the visualization and recitation of Vajrsattva, we can purify these misdeeds, obscurations, and habitual patterns and clear away the veils that make it difficult to remain in rigpa.

In Atiyoga, the main point is to remain within the recognition of awareness. While reading the text, the expression of awareness will be perfectly able to understand the meaning of the words and manifest the visualization, without losing the continuity of awareness itself. In manifesting both Samantabhadra and Chemchok Heruka, know that the seed syllables and the mantra garlands are within the heart centers of both deities. By this, you perfect the offerings to the buddhas and the blessings for all sentient beings in one instant.

> Rays of light radiate and return, accomplishing the two benefits.§

Rays of light radiate up from the seed syllables and letters of the Hundred Syllable mantra and present pleasing offerings to the body, speech, and mind of all buddhas in the infinite buddha fields. The blessings and the accomplishments of the infinite mandala of buddhas return to you in the form of light.

Again, light shines forth to the beings of the six realms and purifies their misdeeds, obscurations, and habitual tendencies. This is called *accomplishing the two benefits*. Presenting offerings upwardly to all the buddhas and receiving the blessings is the benefit for you; downwardly purifying the obscurations of all sentient beings is the benefit for others.

> Spontaneously purifying violations, breaches, and conceptual obscurations.§

When the light returns and is re-absorbed back into you, imagine that all your violations, breaches, and conceptual obscurations are purified, like the morning rays of the sun dissolving the frost on the grass. Violations and breaches refer to the samayas. Conceptual obscurations are thoughts, such as maintaining an observer, an observation, and an object observed. Conceptual obscurations can be gross, subtle, or extremely subtle. As long as these obscurations are not purified, one's recognition of the genuine view remains unstable.

Spontaneously purifying, or purified within the state, refers to the state of primordial purity. All *violations, breaches, and conceptual obscurations* are purified within the recognition of awareness.

Develop the confidence that through the practice of deity, mantra, and samadhi, all misdeeds, breaches, and obscurations, accumulated since beginningless time, are actually purified. Have confidence in the strength of this practice.

Awareness itself is beyond arising, dwelling, and ceasing. Within awareness, there is no degeneration of samaya, no misdeed, and no obscuration. Within awareness, there is no thinker, thought, or object of thinking. It is a space-like state. You cannot paint space; paint does not stay within space. Similarly, thoughts, misdeeds, and obscurations cannot arise within the recognition of awareness.

Within recognition, all former misdeeds are spontaneously purified, the base for future misdeeds is destroyed, and present misdeeds do not manifest—as there is no fixation. The stream of misdeeds is interrupted, as the continuity of thoughts is disconnected.

If you can remain for merely a couple of seconds within awareness, countless aeons of misdeeds are naturally purified; awareness is that powerful. Therefore, remaining within the essence is the king of confessions.

> The world and beings appear as the display of deities, mantras, and wisdom[§]
> Of the all-encompassing peaceful and wrathful ones[§].

Imagine that the world has been transformed into the buddha realm of the *all-encompassing peaceful and wrathful deities.* In addition, visualize that the inhabitants of all six classes have turned into the body, speech, and mind of the peaceful and wrathful deities. In other words, everything dawns as *the display of deity, mantra, and wisdom.* All perceptions are the mandala of deities, all sounds are the mandala of mantra, and all thoughts are the mandala of mind. Within the all-pervading state of primordial purity, there is not even a dust mote of impurity. *All-encompassing* means "beyond any limit or measure."

Because the mandala of the peaceful and wrathful deities is complete within your body, chant the mantra of the forty-two peaceful deities,

OM BODHICHITTA MAHA SUKHA JNANA DHATU AH

and also the mantra for the fifty-eight wrathful deities,

OM RULU RULU HUNG BHYO HUNG

Understand that all of these deities are included within Vajrasattva, and that all mantras are included within the Vajrasattva mantra. By leaving your mind in the natural, uncontrived state, you have practiced all the types of samadhi. All the different deities are in essence Vajrasattva. He is like the single sun within space, reflected within many pools of water. In that same fashion, all deities are the display of the single wisdom.

When chanting, recite the Hundred Syllables a minimum of twenty-one times, as I said earlier, then the short mantra OM BENZA SATO AH. After this, chant the two mantras for the peaceful and wrathful ones, one hundred times each. They can be chanted separately or combined into one mantra. It is perfectly all right to combine the Bodhichitta and the Rulu Rulu mantras into one.

Chant the mantras so that they are audible to you. Generally, peaceful mantras should be chanted audibly and wrathful mantras should be recited under the breath. But here, the mantras are not considered to be wrathful mantras, so you may chant them with a soft voice, audible to yourself. You can also chant the combined Bodhichitta and Rulu Rulu mantras a couple of times in a loud and melodious voice.

While slowly reading the text, do all the necessary visualizations. Briefly visualize the two HUNG syllables, each of the mantra garlands, and the lights radiating out and being re-absorbed again, as you read along. While chanting the mantras, recognize the essence and leave your mind in naturalness. Chant the mantras with your mouth, while your mind rests in naturalness. The chanting of the mantras does not require any thinking whatsoever.

From time to time, remember the visualization, thinking, "I am Vajrasattva." Immediately, look at the thinker of that thought and rest in the recognition of buddha nature. Understand clearly that it is not necessary to maintain a conceptual visualization all the time.

At the completion of the mantra recitations, you may amend omissions and additions during the recitation by reciting the vowels and consonants once. Then stabilize the blessings with one recitation of the Quintessence of Causation. Next, offer confession by reciting the Hundred Syllable mantra once. After this, you can insert the short invitation, offering, praises, and confession beginning with HUNG Yeshe Lhatsog[xi] and so forth. Finally, at the end, dissolve the deity by saying HUNG three times.

Say HUNG HUNG HUNG to dissolve in luminosity.[g]

To reiterate, when first visualizing Vajrasattva, always start out with the suchness samadhi, the dharmakaya. Then, naturally manifest compassion, the all-illuminating samadhi, the sambhogakaya. The seed-syllable samadhi, the nirmanakaya, is the visualization of Vajrasattva's body. Any visualization should always develop out of the three kayas.

When dissolving the visualization, the deity dissolves back into the dharmakaya. Understand this to happen in the following way. While saying HUNG three times, the nirmanakaya Vajrasattva dissolves back into the space of sambhogakaya. The sambhogakaya Vajradhara dissolves back into the space of the dharmakaya. Samantabhadra is the profound and luminous primordial purity, the dharmakaya. The entire visualization dissolves back into the space-like state of Samantabhadra.

When you began the sadhana, you first developed the deity, mantra, and samadhi of Vajrasattva. Now, at the sadhana's completion, when you say HUNG three times, the deity, mantra, and samadhi of Vajrasattva dissolve back into the space of primordial purity. Imagine that the whole universe and its inhabitants, which you formerly visualized as pure sight, sound, and awareness, are now dissolving back into Vajrasattva. Vajrasattva, in turn, along with all the internal deities, dissolves back into the syllable HUNG within Samantabhadra's heart. The syllable HUNG then dissolves from the bottom up to the top and vanishes into emptiness, the space of dharmakaya. Rest some time in the natural state.

When you first developed the deity, you began with the recognition of the dharmakaya, out of which the sambhogakaya naturally manifested. From the sambhogakaya, the visible nirmanakaya manifested in the form of Vajrasattva; now, when dissolving the deity, the visible nirmanakaya dissolves first into the sambhogakaya, and then the sambhogakaya into the dharmakaya.

> Then say PHAT PHAT PHAT to emerge as the deity of the
> post-meditation.⁸

After having dissolved the deity, you need to re-emerge as the deity. While saying PHAT three times, re-emerge in the form of Vajrasattva by thinking, "My nature is Vajrasattva. I am Vajrasattva." In doing this, you manifest again out of dharmakaya as sambhogakaya, and out of sambhogakaya, as the nirmanakaya in the form of Vajrasattva.

The reason for doing this is to clear away the two wrong views of eternalism and nihilism. Eternalism is the view that the universe and all beings are real and have been created by a god. Nihilism is the view that the universe and all beings are really nonexisting and that there is neither karma nor previous or future lives. If you stray into one of these wrong views, then the unified level of Vajradhara is out of reach.

In order to eliminate these two wrong views, dissolve the visualization into emptiness. Through that, the thought of a created and existing universe is cleared away. When re-emerging as the deity Vajrasattva, the thought that nothing exists is also cleared away. By dissolving and re-emerging in this fashion, you eliminate the two wrong views of eternalism and nihilism. When, in fact these two wrong views are eliminated, you will achieve enlightenment, the unified level of Vajradhara, in this very life.

Having re-emerged in the form of the deity at the end of the session, you chant the dedication aspiration.

> Through this merit, may I swiftly⁸
> Accomplish Vajrasattva.⁸

Merit here refers to the merit you have accumulated through this recitation and meditation of Vajrasattva, the practice of deity, mantra, and samadhi. Pray, "May I quickly accomplish Vajrasattva through the merit accumulated today with this practice."

And place every being without exception.§

Make the wish that every sentient being of the six realms of samsara will achieve the level of Vajrasattva.

In that very state.§

By making this wish, you complete both the dedication of merit and the aspiration. Making this dedication and aspiration at the end of the session is the conceptual ending of the sadhana.

When you dedicate the merit, maintain the confidence that you actually have gathered inconceivable amounts of merit. Be aware that you have been practicing the deity, the mantra, and the samadhi of Vajrasattva. Think that you actually have reached and benefited all sentient beings through this dedication. It is very important that you have this kind of confidence in the blessings and power of the practice of deity, mantra, and samadhi.

This conceptual dedication and aspiration should be sealed by the recognition of the nonconceptual awareness. As soon as you have chanted the dedication and aspiration, rest a moment in the nonconceptual state, without the thought of a dedicator, the merit to be dedicated, or beings as the recipients of this dedication. This is called "resting in the nonconceptual state of threefold purity."

Throughout all daily activities, continue the recollection of yourself as being Vajrasattva, maintaining the practice of short glimpses, repeated many times.

Everything is included in this practice, where there is just a single deity, Vajrasattva, a single mantra, OM BENZA SATO AH, and a single samadhi, which is the recognition of your own mind essence. When Guru Rinpoche concealed this text as a terma-treasure, he foresaw that the practitioners of the future would prefer short sadhanas. In the old days, people liked extensive sadhanas. This particular practice is extremely short and easy to do, and it contains swift blessings.

Your chosen yidam deity comprises both the kaya and wisdom aspects of the buddha nature. The kayas and wisdoms are inherently present within the essence of buddha nature. You will swiftly actualize them, when you are able to perform this yidam sadhana in conjunction with Trekchö. Without doubt, the practice of the yidam deity is a great enhancement for Trekchö. The skillful and kind methods of Vajrayana allow us to swiftly accomplish the kayas and wisdoms.

This little sadhana of Vajrasattva is a complete practice. It contains the essence of all the teachings taught in the *Kangyur, Tengyur,* and *Nyingma Gyäbum.* You practice one single deity and one single mantra.

• • •

This was adapted from the Tukdrub Sheldam Nyingjang *by Mangala, Kyabje Dilgo Khyentse Rinpoche.*

Daily Practice of Vajrasattva[55]

*The Various Steps of the Heart Sādhana of Vajrasattva,
Arranged Like a Stream for Recitation Practice,*
[from the Sādhana of Vajrasattva's Enlightened Mind]

EXTRACTED BY *Padma Garwang Tsal*

NAMO VAJRASATTVAYA!
Homage to the enlightened teacher Vajrasattva!

In the main text, it is said,
Someone with faith, diligence, wisdom, and compassion, wishing to follow the authentic and supreme path, should practice the Sādhana of Vajrasattva's Enlightened Mind.
For those wishing to practice essentially, there are three parts: the preliminary, main, and concluding parts.

Preliminaries

Purify your mindstream:

Lama rigdzin gyalwa shyitrö kyilkhor gyi lhatsok tamché dün gyi namkhar

The entire assembly of deities, lamas, awareness-holders, and victorious ones of the peaceful and wrathful mandalas appears in space before me.

---

55 Shechen Publications. 1989. Anything in between [ ] has been added by Han Kop

Powerful Transformation

BENZA SAMA DZAḤ

Thus, do the invocation:

Lama palden dorjé semḥ
Glorious Lama Vajrasattva,

Chok sum gyalwa sé ché laḥ
The Three Jewels, buddhas, and bodhisattvas,

Namkün tü dé chaktsal shyingḥ
To all of you, I prostrate in obeisance,

Chinang chöpa gyatsö chöḥ
Presenting infinite outer and inner offerings.

Dikpa lé ni dok gyi shyingḥ
Turning away from all my evils,

Sönam kün la jé yi rangḥ
I rejoice in all that is good and fortunate

Taktu chökhor korwa dangḥ
And request you to continuously turn the wheel of Dharma

Dro né bardu shyuk leduḥ
And remain as long as beings exist.

Dak ni güp. solwa debḥ
Thus I pray with devotion.

Sönam gang dé khanyam droḥ
Through this merit, may all the innumerable beings

Lamé changchub né tob shokḥ
Attain unsurpassed enlightenment!

Recite this three times or more. Then say:

BENZA MUḤ

Tsok shying nam rang la timpar gyur

Powerful Transformation

Consider that through this, the refuge tree totally dissolves into you.

Main Part

The main part has three sections: the creation of the samayasattva mandala, invitation and empowerment from the jnanasattva mandala, and the recitation practice.

The Creation of the Samayasattva Mandala

OM MAHA SHUNYATA JNANA BENZA SVABHAVA ATMA KO HANG:

Khordé chö kün döma né:
From the very beginning, all the phenomena of samsara and nirvana are

Makyé tongpé ngang nyi lé:
The sphere of unborn emptiness.

Gakmé nyingjé rolpa ni:
From it, the display of unobstructed compassion arises.

Namkha lé ni shyatsön shyin:
Like a rainbow appearing in the sky,

Ngömé ngöpö yeshe trin:
The cloud of wisdom physically manifests yet without substance,

Mingyur hung gi ngowor shar:
Arises as the unchanging nature of HUNG.

Dé lé ö trö choktsam kün:
It radiates light in all directions,

Shyommé dorjé rawa gur:
Establishing the tent of the unbreachable vajra fence,

Yeshe mepung barwé trik:
Which is covered by a mass of blazing wisdom fire.

Dé ü é yam ram bam lam sum:
In the midst of it, from (the syllables) E YAM RAM PAM LAM SUM,

Lé namkha lung mé chu:
Arise the (mandalas of) space, wind, fire, water, and earth.

Sa kyil rirab tengdu droom:
In the center of earth is Mount Meru, upon which is the syllable BHRUM.

Yong gyur kunzang shyalmé khang:
BHRUM transforms completely into an immeasurable, completely excellent palace,

Chinang tsennyi yongdzok ü:
Replete with all the outer and inner characteristics.

Sengtri pema dawé teng:
In the center of this, resting on a lion throne, lotus, and moon disc,

Rigpa hung lé dorjer gyur:
Is the HUNG of awareness, which transforms into a vajra.

Trodü daknyi chomdendé:
Through the emanation and absorption (of rays of light), the vajra becomes the Bhagavan himself,

Dorjé sempa dawé dok:
Vajrasattva, with moon-colored radiance,

Shyi dzum tsen dang pejé bar:
In peaceful aspect, splendid with major and minor marks.

Chak yé dorjé tukkar dzin:
His right hand holds a dorje at heart level,

Yönpa drilbu ku la ten:
His left hand holds a bell with a nine-spoked handle,

Shyab nyi dorjé kyiltrung chen:
And his two legs are in vajra posture.

Pang du nyemma driguk dang:
Dorje Nyema embraces him on his lap,

Töpa dzinpé gul né khyü:
Holding a curved knife and skull cup.

Dar chang rinchen chöpen sok:
Clad in trailing silks with jewelled diadems

Gyenché chusum dak dangden:
And the rest of the thirteen ornaments and garments,

Tayé özer trowa o:
They radiate endless rays of light.

Detar yongsu salwar gyurpé chiwor om karpo

Clearly visualizing this, I imagine that on the forehead is a white OM,

Drinpar ah marpo

In the throat is a red AH,

Nyingkhar hung ngönpo nam kyi tsenpa lé deshyin shekpa
Tamché kyi dorjé sum gyi ngowor gyurpar gyur

And at the heart center is a blue HUNG. These syllables are the very nature of the three vajras (body, speech, and mind) of all the tathagatas.

Invitation and Empowerment from the Jnanasattva Mandala

Consider:

Nyinggé sabön lé jungwé özer gyi yeshe kyi khorlo dün gyi namkhar

By rays of light arising from the seed syllable in my heart as Vajrasattva, the mandala of primordial wisdom is invited in the space before me.

Benza sama dza

Om chok chu kün na lek shyukpé:
Om! All the conquerors and the sons

Chomden gyalwa khor ché kün:
Of the victorious ones dwelling in the ten directions,

Tukjé chenpö gong dzö la:
Think of me with your great compassion,

Mönlam wang gi shek su sol:
And by the power of this prayer, please come here.

E hya hi maha karunika trishya hoh

Samaya hoh:

Samaya tam:

This is the invitation.
Say:

Dza hung bam hoh

The wisdom deities, who are pleased, are thus summoned, bound, and seated.

Om hung tram hri ah:

Abhikhentsa hung:

Om trung benza tukha hoh:

Shyé wangkurwé drima tamché jang

Thus, the initiation purifies all stains,

Pungpo nga né gyur

Completely transforming my five skandhas.

Chü lhakma gyendu lüpa lé deshyin shekpa rik ngé ugyen yeshe nga ngön du gyur

The remainder of the liquid overflows upward, crowning my head with the buddhas of the five families. I take pride in having actualized the five wisdoms.

The Recitation Practice

Dak gi nyinggar ö ngé long:
In my heart, in the midst of five-colored light,

Da teng rang dré yeshepé:
The wisdom being, in a form identical to mine, is seated on a moon.

Tukkar dorjé tewar hung:
In his heart is a vajra, at the center of which is a white HUNG,

Karsal ngak kyi trengwé kor:
Encircled by the radiant, white mantra-rosary.

O trö pak chö jinlab dü:
Lights are radiated to the exalted ones as an offering, and then gathered back as blessings;

Semchen dribdral dechen kö:
The obscurations of sentient beings are purified, and they are established in a state of great bliss.

Tsur dü ngak treng nyi la shyuk:
(The lights) are collected back, and enter into the mantra garland itself.

With one-pointed concentration, recite as much as possible:

OM BENZA SATO AH:

Then, once again, recite:

Om vajra sattva samaya: manu palaya: vajra sattva tvenopa: tishtha dridho mebhava: sutoshyo mebhava: suposhyo mebhava: anu rakto mebhava: sarva siddhi

Powerful Transformation

me prayaccha⃰ sarva karma suchame⃰ chittam shre yam⃰ kuru hung⃰ ha ha ha ha hoh⃰ bhagavan⃰ sarva tathagata⃰ vajra mame munca⃰ vajri bhava⃰ maha samaya sattva ah⃰ hung pe⃰

OM VAJRA SATTVA SAMAYA⃰ MANU PALAYA⃰ VAJRA SATTVA TVENOPA⃰ TISHTHA DRIDHO MEBHAVA⃰ SUTOSHYO MEBHAVA⃰ SUPOSHYO MEBHAVA⃰ ANU RAKTO MEBHAVA⃰ SARVA SIDDHI ME PRAYACCHA⃰ SARVA KARMA SUCHAME⃰ CHITTAM SHRE YAM⃰ KURU HUNG⃰ HA HA HA HA HOH⃰ BHAGAVAN⃰ SARVA TATHAGATA⃰ VAJRA MAME MUNCA⃰ VAJRI BHAVA⃰ MAHA SAMAYA SATTVA AH⃰ HUNG PHAT⃰

At the end of all recitation sessions, say:

Om, palden dorjé sempa kyé⃰
OM! O, glorious Vajrasattva,

Dak la jesu chakpar dzö⃰
Treasure me with your love!

Kyé ga na dang chiwa sok⃰
Protect me from birth, old age, illness, and death,

Jikrung sipé dukngal lé⃰
And from all the fearful suffering of existence.

Gönpo khyö kyi dak kyob shik⃰
You, the protector!

Dikpa kün lé namdrol shying⃰
Liberate me completely from all defilements.

Yangdak yeshe sempa ché⃰
May the utterly pure, great wisdom beings'

Ku sung tuk su dak drub shik⃰
Body, speech, and mind be accomplished in me!

SAMAYA SIDDHI A LA LA HOH⃰

Thus, pray.

The Dissolution Yoga

Rang gi nyinggé ö kyi pokpé kyilkhor gyi khorlo ö du shyu né daknyi damtsik sempa la tim dé yeshe sempa la tim dé ting ngé dzinsem pa la tim deyang hung la tim hung na dé bardu rimgyi tim né mimik pa lé ösal tongpanyi kyi ngang du

Rays of light from my heart center strike the mandala circle. Melting into light, it dissolves into me, the samayasattva, who dissolves into the jnanasattva, who dissolves into the samadhisattva, who dissolves into the HUNG. The HUNG gradually dissolves up to the nada, which dissolves into the nonconceptual state, radiant emptiness. I then rest in meditation.

The Concluding Stages

OM BENZA SATO AH

Lar yang dorjé sempé kur gyurpé

Again, I arise in the form of Vajrasattva.

The Investiture: "Donning the armor," say:

Chiwor om drinpar ah nyinggar hung yik nam kyi tsenpar gyur

At my crown center, throat center, and heart center appear the syllables OM AH HUNG.

Touch the three places with a vajra. Say:

BENZA KA WA TSI RAKSHA HAM

Make the armor-seal mudra at the forehead center and say:

Tamché malü ku sung tuk

Everything without exception is (enlightened) body, speech, and mind;

Ku sung tuk kyi kün la khyab

Vajra body, speech, and mind pervade all.

Thus develop vajra pride.
Conclude with dedications, aspirations, and prayers for auspiciousness, in the usual way.

• • •

I, Padma Garwang Tsal, extracted this from the main text, so I and others could easily put it into practice.

Vajrasattva Drubchen[56]

Orgyen Tobgyal Rinpoche

As the Vajrayana teachings are present and we have met them, we need to practice them. The essence of the tantras is the sadhana section, which is to be practiced. There are four sections of [development stage] practice: approach, close approach, accomplishment, and great accomplishment. Now we are doing a drubchen, and the tradition of drubchen first started here—at Mount Malaya, in English known as Adam's Peak, Sri Lanka—and slowly reached to King Ja and other places. Through the practice of drubchen, great accomplishment, one can progress through the stages of the four vidyadhara levels and reach enlightenment.

In a drubchen, there's a lot to do; it's an elaborate practice, with many details. In the past, there were times when they would do great accomplishment practice and the entire country would join in. For each feast offering, they would offer one hundred thousand measures of gold. Being such a great, elaborate practice, it also makes the results come quickly. It's like the difference between doing something by yourself and doing it with one hundred people. With one hundred people, it can be done immediately. This is a tradition of practice that went to India, to Uddiyana, to the lands of the Muslims, and also to Tibet. However, the way it's done now in Tibet is just a reflection; it kind of looks like it, but it's not the real way, because we're not able to do it exactly as it should be done. So, we're doing the best we can to emulate that and as a mere resemblance, we practice for seven days. Still, this has enormous benefit; the teachings explain how incredible the benefits of such practice are.

---

56 Translated by Marcia B Schmidt

The very essence, the core, of all the tantra and sadhana section teachings is Vajrasattva. In the tantra teachings, it is the essence of Vajrasattva that manifested all the deities, the mandalas, and the teachings. The root of all the sadhanas is Vajrasattva, who gathers into one family the three, five, and one hundred families. They all come down to the one single family of Vajrasattva. The ultimate fruition is to reach the state of Vajrasattva. The great emptiness, the great purity, free of all stains and obscurations, is Vajrasattva. This is the drubchen that we're going to do, the practice of Vajrasattva called *Mindroling Dorsem*, which brings the essence of all the tantra and sadhana sections.

We need to accomplish Vajrasattva. You all have entered the path, of Vajrayana already; now you have no choice. It is something to think about carefully beforehand, before doing it, because it is dangerous. If everything goes well and you keep your samayas, you reach enlightenment very quickly. If everything does not go well and you break your samayas, then you will end up in the worst hell, which means an enormous amount of suffering. Those are the only two options. The main aspect is empowerment. Whether you enter the path of Vajrayana depends on whether you have received empowerment or not. You do have the freedom to decide whether you are going to receive an empowerment or not. Tibetans don't have the slightest doubt; when an empowerment is given, they flock to the empowerment place and receive the empowerment. Many of you Westerners have received empowerment already.

The life force of the empowerment is the samaya. There are samayas of body, speech, and mind; there are the twenty-five samayas and one hundred thousand samayas. Having gotten an empowerment, some people sometimes say, "Oh, don't talk about the samayas, because people will be freaked out." That is the worst thing I've ever heard, because that's a one-way ticket to hell, for sure. About samayas, we don't keep most of them, actually. In general, that's the situation; we actually break more samayas than we keep. That is why Vajrasattva gave this Hundred Syllable mantra, which is the most powerful way of restoring samayas. Vajrasattva, himself, said that if you recite the Hundred Syllable mantra one hundred and eight times without distraction, then all the negativity, all the samaya breakages you may have done, will all be cleansed and purified. Vajrasattva is not a liar. That means that reciting this mantra has enormous benefit. However, first, you need to be able to do it well, correctly.

Powerful Transformation

What is difficult is to be undistracted—which basically means you recite the mantra, visualize the deity, think of the meaning, and leave the mind undistracted. If, on the other hand, you recite the mantra and you're just thinking of all sorts of things, that's when the mind is distracted.

You need to be undistracted, and that is how to do the drubchen as much as you can. Practice the self-visualization, the front visualization, and the vase visualization. Actualize body [appearances as the deity], speech as mantra, mind in samadhi, the emanating, and reabsorbing. After that come the fulfillment and confession practices, in which you apologize and repair by fulfillment, which has four sections. Following that is the self-empowerment, through which you stabilize the wisdom you received at the time of the empowerment. First you receive the empowerment from the lama and every day you restore that through the self-empowerment. Next comes the feast offering. When you do all these practices, you should be undistracted, because if you are distracted that won't bring much result. Think well about this.

Now, actually when teaching about drubchen, one needs to talk about all the aspects of development stage practice. There are many sections in development stage practice; there are the preliminaries, the main part, and the concluding sections. I've taught quite extensively about this in the past.[xii] Now is the time to put all these into practice, and the way to do so boils down to sights, sounds, and samadhi. All appearances manifest as the deity, all sounds as mantra, and all thoughts as awareness. Do this for seven days; however, the nail[xiii] of unchanging wisdom mind, is not something that we are able to keep for seven days. Again and again renew it, [rest in the nail of unchanging wisdom mind]; it gets lost and repeatedly bring it back. To put it concisely, ordinary thoughts decrease and development stage practice increases.

• • •

If you don't know the practice, you need to bring in the four powers. The drubchen starts later today, so think, "before beginning this drubchen, for countless aeons, I have accumulated bad karma, evil deeds, and negative emotions; things have not turned out well." We really need to have regret. Of course, you could think, "I haven't done anything negative," but you are still in samsara. We are deluded and every instant we accumulate so much negativity. In particular, we forget about the vows of individual liberation, the greater vehicle trainings in bodhichitta, and the Vajrayana samaya precepts. There are also the ten unvirtuous actions we have done. And it is not just you, but all sentient beings have done that. We need to develop regret, and we are not going to lose anything by doing it; just have that sense of regret.

First is the power of regret. Once you have generated regret, it is necessary to confess those negative actions. You also need to purify them through confession. For the confession to work, you need to have regret, because otherwise it becomes like the way Westerners say sorry all the time, but don't really mean it. To have regret without formal confession practice is fine, but you can't have confession without regret. When offering confession, we need a support. For the drubchen, we've established the mandala of Vajrasattva, indivisible from Vajrasattva as the support. Actually, the glory of Vajrasattva appears, wherever you want it to appear, because the body of Vajrasattva is the space-like wisdom body; like space, it is absolutely everywhere. That is the support for confession, this elaborate mandala we've erected. Then you need to make the pledge not to make future negative actions and do the best you can. This benefits a bit. Westerners have the expression, "I did my best!" So do your best. However, just to say it is not good enough; really think well about doing it.

The key point is that you meditate on the deity Vajrasattva and the mandala, make the offerings, engage in the ritual, and invite the wisdom deity. With this support, confess negative actions and make the pledge that in future, [you will not do them]. This will ensure that negative actions are purified, based on these methods. Really be able to decide that this is so. You need to have stable devotion. Whether your devotion is stable has to do with whether you've been able to decide clearly or not. Decide definitively that through the power of the deity, mantra, and samadhi, then all negativity has been purified. Otherwise, if you are unsure, then you are fooling yourself. If you are fooling yourself, what benefit is there? You need trust; that is the most important point, so think well about this.

Whether there's benefit for you or not basically has to do with your mind; the dharma is about the mind. Even if physically you are unable to put in much effort, at least, if you put effort into your mind and apply

Powerful Transformation

these points, there will be some benefit. If not, if you just come to all the sessions, stay for the night sessions, and exhaust yourself, all the while thinking about all sorts of things, that is a waste of time. It would be better to stay in your bed and sleep!

. . .

Now comes a brief explanation on how to engage in this practice. Ultimate bodhichitta is emptiness, one's own mind, beyond thought, word, and expression. Based on emptiness in Vajrayana, the clarity of the empty mind arises as the deity. There is body, speech, and mind. Body is apparent, speech is semi-apparent, and mind is nonapparent. The body that is appearing now is our ordinary body, and we need to meditate on the pure body of Vajrasattva, as described in the text.

The text says,

OM MAHA SHUNYATA JNANA BENZA SVABHAVA ATMA KO HANG.

These are the words that establish emptiness. All things of samsara and nirvana are emptiness. Within emptiness, all phenomena of samsara and nirvana unfold: *From the very beginning, all the phenomena of samsara and nirvana are the sphere of unborn emptiness*. Then the text leads to the three samadhis. This is a very vast topic that I do not have time to go into here. In short, they are the samadhi of suchness, the illuminating samadhi, and the samadhi of the seed syllable, which you need to meditate on. The third samadhi is the samadhi of the seed syllable; here, it's the letter HUNG. As you progress through the text, there is the outer world and the inner contents of beings; the outer world is the palace, and within the palace is the seat. All of this is indivisible from your own mind. The letter HUNG descends onto the seat and transforms into a vajra, from which light radiates out, making offerings to the buddhas and reabsorbing as blessings. Once again, light goes out and the vajra transforms into Vajrasattva. Vajrasattva is very clearly described in the text. If that is too complicated, each of you has a photo of Vajrasattva that you can study. Vajrasattva is the lord of all families. It is the one family that includes the nature of all families. If you accomplish Vajrasattva, you accomplish all deities, as when you turn on the main switch, all the lights go on.

When meditating on Vajrasattva, you need vivid presence, stable pride, and pure recollection. Visualize Vajrasattva in union with his consort, skillful means and wisdom inseparable; that is the meditation. Keep following the text, which says, *By rays of light arising*. It is necessary to begin with a self-visualization. In the Nyingma tradition, there is no division between self-visualization and front-visualization; they are together. Here, first do a self-visualization and after this is finished, you, the samayasattva, then invite the wisdom being. After the wisdom being takes his seat, you make offerings and praises. These are all the different aspects of a sadhana. When we do sadhana, we need the mudras and the samadhis. It is easy to see others doing the mudras and imitate. Now we have our ordinary, impure body, and these are all methods of purifying.

Next comes the speech-recitation section, as in the text: Within my heart as the samayasattva, is *the wisdom being, in a form identical to mine*. In the heart of the wisdom being, or jnanasattva, is a vajra, which is the samadhisattva, with a HUNG inside it, encircled by the mantra. Light rays go out, make offerings, and bring back the blessings and siddhis. All four recitation intents are here: the moon with the garland of stars, the firebrand, the messenger of the king, and the beehive broken open; nothing is left out. While reciting, think about these. The condensed mantra is OM BENZA SATO AH. OM BENZA SATO SAMAYA and so on, is the extensive mantra. For the meaning of the Hundred Syllable mantra, you can study Jamyang Khyentse Wangpo's[xiv] explanation of this mantra. The mantra is in Sanskrit, and if you do not know Sanskrit, you can recite many times but not know the meaning. The Hundred Syllable mantra itself is not most important. What is important is the meaning; it is good to look at the meaning. But if you still cannot understand that, then supplicate Vajrasattva; invoke the wisdom mind of Vajrasattva.

When reciting the Hundred Syllables, we are performing the speech aspect, and through recitation, we realize vajra speech. At the time of recitation think, "All appearances are the deity, [enlightened body]; all sound is mantra, [enlightened speech]; and all thoughts are the display of unchanging wisdom mind. Everything—the three realms, the container and contents, beings—is the nature of enlightened mind. So like this, the sadhana is a self-visualization, then there is the dissolution and re-emergence. The words are as follows:

Rays of light from my heart center strike the mandala circle. Melting into light, it dissolves into me, the samayasattva, who dissolves into the jnanasattva, who dissolves into the samadhisattva, who dissolves into the HUNG. The HUNG gradually dissolves up to the nada, which dissolves into the nonconceptual state, radiant emptiness; I then rest in meditation.

Then rest in that and when a thought arises, do not regard it as an ordinary thought; it is your re-emergence as Vajrasattva. The text says, OM BENZA SATO AH. Thus bring forth the clear visualization of Vajrasattva again.

There is a front-visualization, which is more detailed. The self-visualization is the terma text itself, revealed by Terdak Lingpa, who expanded on the terma with the more detailed visualization. What might have happened is that students were unclear about the shorter text, so he added all the details. For example, the palace is explained, with its pillars, doors, and decorations. Also in the front visualization, each ornament on Vajrasattva is listed, where the ornaments are merely mentioned in the terma text. The offerings are more elaborate. However, the practice is the same. Now, we have reached the self-visualization and the front-visualization in this practice. During recitation, rays of light radiate from the self-visualization and go the heart of the front-visualization and emanate. The main effort involves the front-visualization.

Next is the blessing of the vase. Meditate on Vajrasattva inside the vase and recite the mantra. From the self-visualization, light rays dissolve into the vase; these light rays are like sweat. Finally, Vajrasattva turns into light that dissolves into the amrita [in the vase]. Now we have completed three visualizations, self, front, and vase, which are the same. There is not a big retinue, only Vajrasattva; there aren't many different mantras, just the Hundred Syllables and its essence mantra, OM BENZA SATO AH.

We have arrived at the self-initiation; it is an empowerment. From the dharmakaya Buddha Samantabhadra until our own root guru is an unbroken lineage, which is the lineage empowerment. The path empowerment needs to be taken every day, as to not deteriorate and to revitalize the lineage with the lama. When we become enlightened, in the future, we will have the fruition empowerment. In this practice, there is the path empowerment, the self-empowerment. The tradition in India is that before you do any work, you need to wash, like washing your hands before eating. Likewise, before receiving the self-empowerment, we need to cleanse. We also need to offer a mandala, which is extremely important. Then we request the yidam to bestow the empowerment followed by refuge, developing bodhichitta, and the Vajrayana vows. Unless we think, "I am going to keep the vows," we cannot get the empowerment. Lately people want the empowerment but do not want the samayas. So, we commit to the samayas.

The empowerment begins with the view and descent of wisdom, the most important part. One visualizes oneself as Vajrasattva in union with a consort and many wisdom beings are invoked and dissolve into oneself. We request the wisdom beings to remain until we become enlightened and we seal it with placing the vajra on our head. Next comes the request for the four empowerments, so once again we offer a mandala. We are following the intent of the tantras. The four empowerments are the vase, the secret, the wisdom knowledge, and the precious word empowerments. The vajra master, inseparable from the main deity of the mandala, bestows the empowerment on the students, who recognize this. We receive all four empowerments and even though we have received the lineage empowerment before, to prevent degeneration, we renew and stabilize that transmission. Think this and have the confidence that it is so. Once we have taken the four empowerments, we vow to keep the samayas. The life force of the empowerment is the samayas, and if we do not keep them, then the life force is severed.

Once again, we offer a mandala—not just a mandala, we offer everything, our body and our possessions. This represents how the dharma is greater than anything else. In worldly terms, we value things that are the most expensive. By offering our body, possessions, and all our merit, we show how precious this is. Afterwards, we dedicate. This is one cycle of the sadhana practice. According to the Nyingma tradition, the best way to do a drubchen is to do the sadhana three times in the day and three times in the night, six times. If not possible, then at least do four times, two times during the day, and two times during the night. That is what we will do here, because foreigners will have trouble going as quickly as the lamas and monks can.

Progressing through the sadhana, we arrive at the confession, *Yeshe Konchok*. There are many extensive confessions: for example, for body, there are prostrations to the hundred peaceful and wrathful deities; for speech, there is the definitive confession of *Rudra Meshak;* and for mind, there is confession of the view. Offering confession for the body, prostrate; for speech, say the Hundred Syllable mantra; and for mind, meditate. All of this is included in *Narak Kongshak,* whereas in the *Mindroling Dorsem,* the confession is the general confession of *Yeshe Konchok* and the one following that. Once finished with confession, we make the pledge, in order to keep this purification stable. When we are sick and we have finished taking the medicine, we apply methods to not get ill again. It is said in the tantras that there are twenty-eight commitments that we need to keep. These are quite scary; reading them makes me afraid. One has to one-pointedly make these pledges, and we commit to them by holding the vajra at our heart, which is a way to stabilize our vows. After that, there is a short pledge as well. Next come the four fulfillments. The first is in accordance with the view. Thereafter, they are fulfillments of amrita, rakta, torma, and butter lamps. These have incredible meaning. If, in this life, we can truly enact fulfillment, then all broken samayas and transgressions are purified.

Vajrasattva is the lord of the one family, which when expanded is the hundred families. The five poisons are transmuted into the five wisdoms. The peaceful ones abide purely and the wrathful ones transform [from this]. First the peaceful ones abide as naturally pure, [primordially pure] and the wrathful ones are transformed from them, and connected with this are two fulfillment prayers. So, each day, from the confession down through the fulfillment, we recite these verses without break. Best is to do them twice daily. In short, the confession and the fulfillment are extremely important. The Mindroling tradition does not recite the *Narak Kongshak,* but we do. The reason is that we wish to attain enlightenment and we have taken empowerments, and to keep the samayas, we need to confess and fulfill, considering that we are constantly fighting amongst ourselves. There is benefit in doing these.

The root of empowerment is samaya, as I have said, and there are two categories, the root and subsidiary, or branch, samayas. There are fourteen root samayas. The first is not to go against the vajra master,[xv] not to upset or disobey him. The lama is the vajra master. The vajra master can be endowed with one, two, or three kindnesses. The first kindness pertains to the master who bestows empowerment. Having given empowerment, the master with the second kindness also explains the tantras. A master who points out the nature of mind is endowed with the third kindness. We need to cherish the master endowed with the three kindnesses, more than our own hearts. It is one's choice whether you cherish the lama or not and whether you need to. It is necessary to check the master before you receive teachings from him or her and that is merely about any teachings. Regarding empowerments, it is more critical to check the teacher; you need to make sure that they have the proper lineage. To be introduced to mind nature, in Dzogchen, then you really need to investigate the master giving these teachings.

When receiving the vows of the lower vehicle then the abbot who imparts them is like your father, and you are like the child. Buddha Shakyamuni said this in the Vinaya. When you receive the trainings of Mahayana, the lama is like a doctor and the student is like a sick person. If you do not take the medicine and the doctor's advice, you die. For an empowerment, one needs to see the master as indivisible from [the main deity of] the mandala, which is the way to receive the empowerment. If not, you will not really get the empowerment. To truly receive the pointing out instruction, you need to see the master as the Buddha. If you see the teacher as the Buddha, you can be introduced to the mind as the Buddha. This teacher is the most precious and important. Then there are the samayas of the three kayas, and if we go against them, we break them. So, the second root samaya is to abide by whatever instruction the teacher gives you.

The third root samaya concerns the dharma friends,[xvi] and there is a lot to say about this. In fact, buddha nature permeates all beings; we all have the same *gyu* basis. Merely harming even one sentient being is a negative action. That is the larger dharma community; a smaller group is the students of the same teacher. Even closer are those with whom you receive empowerment in one mandala. It becomes increasingly tighter as you receive not only an empowerment but teachings together as well. Then there are those with whom you receive Dzogchen teachings and they are truly your vajra siblings. They are very important and to be treated with respect; there are many texts that explain this. It says that you need to consider each one of them as the lama and explains why you should avoid fighting with them in any manner, not even holding negative thoughts about them in your mind. There are many details and if you do not keep these, you will go to hell. Actually you will go to the worst hell. In sutra it is called Avichi Hell; in Vajrayana, it is called Vajra Hell and you will stay there a very long time, an immeasurable length of time.

These days people do not respect these [samayas] at all. They do try somewhat to keep the samayas with the lama, as long as there are no difficulties. Mentally, you probably think negative things about the lama. But there is no consideration whatsoever for vajra siblings, and that is only the third one, so you can imagine the rest!

What do you do when samayas are broken? There are several levels: damaged, transgressed, and broken, according to time. The quicker you can purify it through confession, the better. Time matters; it matters how long it has been damaged, whether it is a month, days, or weeks. We have the way to confess as illustrated here in this drubchen practice.

We have come to the feast offering, which is the supreme way to purify breakages and remain clean. We need to accumulate both merit and wisdom, and feast offering increases these. We, therefore, make offerings to the dharma protectors, first. We then follow the text all the way to the residual offering, followed by offering the covenant, the *tenma*, and so forth. To prevent obstacles that steal the siddhis from arising, we liberate the *nyuley*[xvii] spirits. In an elaborate fashion, we would do this liberation offering to the nyuley twelve times, corresponding to the twelve different times in the day that the twelve different types of nyuley appear. To liberate each one of them, we need to invoke a specific deity, with a specific mantra, and specific substances to liberate each one. Here we do it more essentially, at the end of each session. If we do not liberate them, the siddhis could get lost.

Having done that, we request the blessings from the deities during the descent of blessings practice, which comes next. At this particular time and place, we are doing the *Descent of Blessings of the Great Sacred Places (Nas chen Jin beb)*, a very extensive descent of blessings invocation, from the sacred places and the beings associated with those places. At a precious site like this, confessing breakages restores the blessings of the site. Quite honestly, this place is a buddhafield; before, it was impossible to even come here, without high realization. But these days the blessings must have declined, as even tourists have arrived.

In this world, the most important, sacred places are those that the nirmanakaya buddha, Shakyamuni, went to: Bodhgaya, Varanasi, Kushinagar, and so forth. The one thousand buddhas will go to those places in this kalpa. In the buddhafield of Akanishtha, the most precious and sacred place, the sambokakaya manifested and then came and taught the secret Vajrayana for the first time here. This was an emanation of Vajrasattva who taught the Vajrayana to those five extraordinary beings. He turned an inconceivable wheel of the teachings for them at this very place.

In order to restore and stabilize the blessings here, at Adam's Peak, we perform this detailed descent of blessings, at the end of the evening session. We invoke all the wisdom deities, yidams, dakinis, the dharma protectors, Guru Rinpoche, and so on to send their blessings. This benefits the doctrine to remain, because if the doctrine is firm, then sentient beings are benefited. This is accomplishing enlightened activities for sentient beings.

When circling the mandala, all the yogis need to wear their ornaments. Actually, they should dress in charnal ground attire, just like the picture of Jamyang Khyentse Lodro dressed that way. If we are not able to wear all those ornaments, then at least we don the hats, the yellow dharma robes, and brocade cloaks. The benefit is that this auspicious connection arranged in the body brings realization to the mind. It is like when we see a Sri Lankan monk dressed in the yellow robes, we know he is a Theravadan monk. As we are in the tradition of Guru Rinpoche, then we wear the crown of Guru Rinpoche and the red dharma robes with golden patterns; when we see this, we see Guru Rinpoche. Actually seeing all the beings in the three realms of existence, we see them as Guru Rinpoche, as they are students of Guru Rinpoche. We recite the mantra and think about the meaning of the prayer. To symbolize the descent of the five wisdoms, we wave streamers of five colored silks. It is a symbol, like the traffic light; when we see red, we stop, and green, we go. The multicolored streamers are an invitation to the five buddha families to arrive and send their blessings. We hold the vajra and the bell to show that we are practitioners of Vajrayana, because Vajrayana practice is the unity of skillful means and wisdom, symbolized by the bell and vajra. We also chant loudly, play the bell and damaru, and sound the trumpets at this point in the ritual. We offer incense and burn *gugul*. These are the special substances that we use. If we do this at a place like this, so precious to the Vajrayana, then it will not only bless this place, it will also extend out to the other twenty-four sacred places and help the Vajrayana doctrine to remain there and be of benefit, as Dakpo Rinpoche explained to me.

I have explained the practice; there are many key points; it is difficult. For the buddha dharma, it is not enough to just think about it—you need to really contemplate upon it. The teacher teaches and the student thinks very well about the teachings. You really need to reflect on them, and to be able to do this, you need to be intelligent. These days, there are not that many smart people. One of the first things to do to be able to understand the Mahayana teachings is to pray to Manjushri to increase intelligence. To understand the buddha dharma requires great intelligence, and the Buddha taught that in the beginning, intelligence is needed for the path.

These days most people are quite dull, like being asleep or drunk; people cannot think. For the secret Vajrayana, there are secret and hidden points that need to be uncovered. No matter how much they are explained, most people do not understand them. If you understand well, buddhahood is very close, and you will be taken away from samsara. Once you understand, you need to experience and then realize it. If you realize it, you are a siddha. This understanding brings you very close. So, what do we need? We need merit. In these degenerate times, only people devoid of merit come to the teachings. However, those who have come here to participate in this drubchen do have great merit. In the whole world, you have the most merit. The person with the most merit was the Buddha; no one has more than he does. Yet, this is not easy. For both Mahayana and Vajrayana, you must not separate from the view, meditation, and action. We think that we need to unite these and we do not do it. Now we are here in this place for seven days. It was not easy to come and it is hard to know how many future opportunities like this will again arise. However, this is even better than going to a party, because one needs to dress up to go to a party, talk to different people, get a bit drunk, and spend a few hours, which is a worldly way. But here, we are at a great party, where we will be together for seven days practicing. We will meditate on the deity, mantra, mudra, and samadhi.

The mandala we set up is not the real mandala but a resemblance. There is the actually present offering and the mentally created ones. I am not sure how much of the mentally created ones we can do, but we will make sure that we have the actually present ones. If we do this correctly, practice with deity, mantra, mudra, and samadhi, then a kalpa of obscurations and negative deeds will be purified. Also, we will accumulate a massive amount of both merit and wisdom. That is what we are doing here, and in the end we will conclude with the butter lamp prayer. I do not know how much of the supreme and common accomplishments we will receive, but at least we will have a great time partying, rejoicing together! This is very good and beneficial.

The Heart of Vajrasattva

The King of Purifications, Taught According to the Stainless Secret of Vajrasattva.

Do Khyentse Yeshe Dorje

OM:
Primordial Buddha Samantabhadra, the ground of being:
Vajrasattva, Vajra Tathagata,:
Lord and great daka who protects beings,:
Kindly consider me and gaze upon me with your wisdom eyes.:

AH:
From the beginning, unborn and primordially pure,:
Yet concepts that arise momentarily in my confused experience:
Cause ignorance, dualistic perception, violations, and breaches.:
I confess all of these in the space of the great, pure dharmadhatu consort.:

VAJRA:
Lord of mysteries, Vajrapani, who proclaims the vajra samaya,:
Whichever of the hundred thousand body, speech, mind, and secret samayas:
I have violated or words I have gone against,:
I feel very ashamed, and with regret I openly admit and confess.:

SATTVA:

Having passed the time limit when violations become faults,
Which are the causes for harsh punishment
At the command of the vajra dakinis, the monitors of karma,
I confess having accumulated the causes of the great hells that obscure this life and the next.

HUNG
King of Passion, great primordial vajra,
Beyond concepts, free from violation and confession,
Samantabhadra, primordially perfect space of awareness,
Beyond meeting and parting, in the dharmadhatu space. AH.

This King of Confessions, in just a few words, can stir samsara from its depths, like alchemy applied to iron. It is an oral instruction to protect beings who have fallen subject to ignorance and samaya violations. It arose from the sphere of the mind of Samantabhadra. I, Padma, wrote it down in symbolic script for the sake of future generations. May it meet with my heart son, an emanation of myself.

Samaya maya budhya shubham

. . .

This was established from the code script by Traktung Pawo (Do Khyentse Yeshe Dorje).

Virtue! Virtue! Virtue!

Appendix

EXTRACTED FROM *The Light of Wisdom*, Volume II

Padmasambhava, Chokgyur Lingpa, Jamgön Kongtrül, and Jokyab Rinpoches

The Effect, Visualizing the Mandala of the Support

Visualizing the Support, the Celestial Palace

The *Lamrim Yeshe Nyingpo* root text says,

> From it radiates glowing light that purifies clinging to concreteness.
> Upon the gradually layered elements, within the expanse of the five consorts,
> Visualize the external world as the great realms of the peaceful and wrathful ones,
> Such as the delightful palace of Glorious Heruka
> As well as the vajra protection circle, charnel grounds, and surroundings,
> And the seat of lotus, sun, moon, haughty spirit, and so forth.

The effect, visualizing the mandala of the support and the supported, has the following general sequence. The purpose is to purify the clinging to the gradual forming of the content-like beings after the vessel-like world is formed. Since the realm in which all tathagatas awaken is the realm of their natural experience, free from all obscurations, and since at the time of the higher paths, you first purify the coarse body and nadi-elements and then gradually control and purify the more subtle speech and pranas and then the mind and bindus, there is a definite sequence of the support and what is supported. For this reason, you must first visualize the mandala that is the support, and this is done in conformity with the gradual way in which the world is formed in the impure state.

The *Galtreng* describes this,

> Visualize the gradual layers and the palace,
> In the manner in which the worlds gradually appear.

How do you visualize this? Imagine that the seed syllable remaining in the middle of space radiates immense glowing rays of light, in the form of fire, wind, and water, which purify all types of clinging to the concreteness of a world and beings, which then become emptiness. The training in emptiness at the time of the previous samadhi of suchness was to purify the inner fixating thoughts, while this [samadhi] is for the specific purpose of purifying the objects of form. Therefore, there is no redundancy.

Next, the objects to be purified are, first, the element of space, which forms the basis for the vessel-like world to be formed and the place for sentient beings to take birth; second, the primary cause for this creation, which is the all-doing mind itself; and finally, the particular habitual tendencies accumulated as the beings' common karma which, when clung to in their minds, ripen into their shared experience of objects and thus form the mandalas of the four elements together with Mount Sumeru.

The method for purifying is to visualize the seed-syllable gradually emanating the syllables. From these, within the space of the source-of-dharmas, gradually visualize the layered four elements of wind, fire, water, and earth, together with their enclosure. The *Magical Display* describes this,

> The outer elements as the consorts and so forth
> Are the nonduality of means and knowledge.[xviii]
> Steadiness is Vajra Lochana,

Powerful Transformation

Liquidity is the goddess Mamaki,
Maturation and burning is Pandara Vasini,
Lightness and motility is the expanse of Tara,
And bright empty space is Samantabhadri.

In this way, to assume the pride of thinking, "The five elements are the five consorts!" will ensure that, as the result of purification, they are purified into being dharmadhatu, the realm in which all buddhas awaken and which has the nature of the five female consorts.

In this way, you are to visualize the celestial palace within the spacious expanse of the five elements, the nature of which is the five consorts. The objects to be purified are the concepts that cling to the items enjoyed in connection with a sentient being's life—homeland, house, possessions, and so forth.

The means of purification is to imagine that from the syllable BHRUM, the essence of Vairochana, appears the peaceful celestial palace of great liberation, or, for the wrathful [deities], the utterly delightful sporting charnel ground that is the great Glorious Heruka's palace of supreme secret.[xix] Visualize the base below, the enclosures on the sides, the dome above, the gates, portals, distinctive ornamentation, and so forth. Outside of these is the vajra protection circle and the landscape of the eight great self-existing charnel grounds. Assume the pride that this is the realm of the celestial palace at the time of fruition.[xx] By doing so, the result of purification is to actualize the abode of buddhahood, the secret great delight of the bhaga of the five vajra queens, which has the nature of unconstructed dharmadhatu.

At the time of the path, the gradually layered elements together with Mount Sumeru are the five nadi-wheels and the central channel. The substructure below the celestial palace, consisting of the vajra cross, lotus and sun, are the pranas and essential elements abiding in the center of these nadi-wheels. The celestial palace is the blissful quality of empty and cognizant mind, intermingled as one taste with all these. Fully training yourself in visualizing this will make the nadis, pranas, and bindus pliant and manageable, and function as the ripening of the higher paths, because it lays the basis for the special wisdom.

The objects to be purified in these [steps] are the concepts of the places in which sentient beings take rebirth: the lotus of the mother as well as the semen and blood of the parents, the heat and moisture, and so forth. The means of purifying these concepts is to train in visualizing the seat consisting of the lotus, sun and moon, in the case of the peaceful; and of the lotus, sun, haughty spirit, animal, and so forth, in the case of the wrathful.[xxi] The result of such purification is the manifestation of the qualities of the rupakayas of buddhahood, in conformity with the symbolized meaning of these seats, such as nonattachment, luminosity, and so forth.[xxii]

At the time of the path, the lotus is the nadi-wheels, the sun is the tummo fire, the moon is the syllable HANG at the crown of the head; and thus they are the melting bliss of the blazing and dripping. Alternatively, the lotus, sun, and moon can respectively be the lotus of the prajna maiden in the center of which dwells the sun of bodhichitta stabilized by the kunda of the male consort. Training yourself in visualizing this will function as the ripening [of the higher paths] because it lays the basis for the tummo at the time of the completion stage and for attaining the unchanging great bliss by means of the mudra activity.

To summarize, the objects to be purified are the ordinary experiences of this world comprised of the outer vessel. The means of purification is to visualize the boundless and immeasurable great realms of the peaceful and wrathful ones densely arrayed with adornments. The result of such purification is to achieve mastery over the buddhas' realm of natural experience, which is beyond center and limits.

Tibetan Source Material

Chokling Tersar[57]
Volume A: Author: Chokgyur Lingpa, (mchog gyur gling pa)

gsang thig snying po'i skor las rdo rje gzhon nu pyag rgya gcig pa'i sgrub thabs ldeb, 35–42
Supplication and The Sadhana of the Single Form of Vajrakilaya

gsang thig snying po'i skor las rdo rje gzhon nu phyag rgya gcig pa'i lha khrid rab gsal khrag 'thug dgyes pa'i gad rgyangs ldeb, 123–149
A Roar to Delight Heruka

Chokling Tersar
Volume HA: Author: Chokgyur Lingpa, (mchog gyur gling pa)

gsang thig snying po'i skor las rdo rje sems dpa' phyag rgya gcig pa'i sgrub thab ldeb, 465–471
The Practice of the Single Form of Vajrasattva

gsang thig snying po'i skor las rdor sems phyag rgya gcig pa'I bskyed rdzogs kyi gnad 'chad par byed pa rdo rje sems sa dpa' zhal lung, 513–539
The Words of Vajrasattva

Volume KI: Author: Chokgyur Lingpa, (mchog gyur gling pa)

rdzogs pa chen po gser gyi zhun gyi sngon 'gro nges legs lam bzang sdeb, 175–185
Extracted from: The Excellent Path to True Goodness

Chokling Tersar
Volume KA: Author: Chokgyur Lingpa, (mchog gyur gling pa)

---

57 Please note, all Chokling Tersar references are from the TBRC editions.

rdor sems rgyun khyer mdor bsdus bzhugs
The Abridged Daily Practice of Vajrasattva
Extracted from *Zhal gdams snying byang*

rdzogs pa chen po gser gyi zhun gyi sngon 'gro nges legs lam bzang sdeb, 175–185
Extracted from: *The Excellent Path to True Goodness*
Visualization and Recitation of Vajrasattva

Rinchen Terdzo, Volume GA: Author Terchen Terdag Lingpa

sMin lugs rdor sems gTer gzhung
sGrub mchod rgyas pa'i lag len
Daily Practice of Vajrasattva
Extracted by Padma Garwang Tsal, [another name for Jamgön Kongtrül]

APPENDIX
Padmasambhava, Chokgyur Lingpa, Jamyang Khyentse Wangpo, Jamgön Kongtrül, and Jamyang Drakpa. *Light of Wisdom,* Volume II. Translated from the Tibetan by Erik Pema Kunsang. (Hong Kong: Rangjung Yeshe Publications, 1995). 72–75.

ENDNOTES

i.   See Commentary by Orgyen Tobgyal Rinpoche.

ii. *The Eight Heruka tantras*, including the *Phurba Tantra*, according to Tulku Urgyen Rinpoche, were from the heart of Khandro Leykyi Wangmo, who manifested a garuda, from which emanated the *Eight Heruka tantras*, which were hidden as terma. [Bo COLOMBY]

iii. These teachings were given by Kyabje Dilgo Khyentse Rinpoche to Ven. Chögön Rinpoche at Dharamsala on 4th of February, 1991. This rough and imperfect translation was made by Konchog Tendzin [MATTHIEU RICARD].

iv. In the arrangement of this practice by Tsikey Chokling Rinpoche, a longevity practice is inserted here that appears in the root terma, but is not explained in the commentary. Additionally, in the root terma, there is vase practice, not included in Tsikey Chokling Rinpoche's arrangement.
Here is the longevity practice of Vajrasattva:

Dorje sempa yabyum gom
Yabkyi tugkar migyur wey
Shelgyi dorje gyadram gyi
Tewar nyidey gau ü
Visualizing Vajrasattva with consort,
In the heart center of the male figure,
In the hub of the changeless crystal vajra-cross,
Amidst the sphere of the sun and moon,
AH NRI HUNG SUM TAMA RU
Ngagkyi trengwey korwa ley
Özer samye tröney su
Tseye barchey tamchey jang
Around the threefold A, NRI, and HUNG,
Coils the mantra garland.
From it radiate boundless rays of light
To purify all hindrances for longevity.
Düsum deshek tamchey kyi

Powerful Transformation

Tugkyi yeshe tsepal dang༈
Lhadang drangsong tamchey kyi༈
Tseyi ngödrub malü dang༈
They gather back the wisdom, life, and splendor༈
Of the minds of all sugatas in the three times,༈
And every siddhi of longevity༈
From all the devas and the rishis.༈
Jungwa zhiyi chünam dang༈
Kyedro namkyi tsesö dang༈
Rangi latsey döngyi kü༈
Dedag tamchey tsurdü tey༈
They gather back the essences of the four elements༈
And the merit and life-energy of all beings.༈
As well as my life and vitality stolen by evil forces.༈
Gathering back all of this,༈
Dütsi ngayi nampa ru༈
Khayi nangdu zhugney su༈
Lükyi nangnam tamchey gang༈
Lüni tragdang ziji den༈
They enter in through my mouth༈
In the form of the five nectars.༈
They fill the whole interior of my body,༈
So the body is majestic and radiant.༈
Ga-u chungzey khajey wey༈
Dangmey dangma chü tamchey༈
Ah nri hung sum la tim pey༈
Tragdang ö-nga barwa dang༈
When the sphere opens slightly༈
All the nectars, the quintessential liquids,༈
Dissolve into the threefold A, NRI, and HUNG,༈
So that their radiance glows with five-colored light.༈
Ga-ü khadrig ögzhi yi༈
Dorje razhi tengdu dü༈
Dorje lugu gyükyi ching༈
Chimey dorjei sogtob gyur༈
The sphere re-joins and the four lower vajra-prongs༈
Tie together at the top༈
And are bound with the vajra chain,༈
So that the vajra life of immortality is attained.༈
OM VAJRA SATTVA AMARANI JIWAN TIYE SVAHA༈

v. In the Vajrayāna, the threefold kindness is explained to be the guru's kindness of conferring empowerment, explaining the tantras, and bestowing oral instructions.

vi. *The Excellent True Goodness,* see sources quoted.

vii. This is referring to Chokgyur Lingpa.

viii. This liturgy for the Eight Branches is as follows:

Ho dorje lobpön sangye pal düsüm shuk la chak tsal lo
Hoh. Vajra master, glorious buddha, abiding throughout the three times, I bow before you.

Chok sum tenpé shying gyur la nyimé yikyi kyab su chi
Free of doubt, I take refuge in those who are the basis for the teachings of the Three Jewels.

Ngö jor yikyi nam trül pé dagpe chopa shye su sol
Please accept these pure offerings, both actually present and mentally created.

Ngödrub chuwo chopé gek nyejé malü shak par gyi
I apologize without exception for all misdeeds, the hindrances that obstruct the river of accomplishment.

Chok chu khor süm dagpé chö ma chak chö la jé yi rang
I rejoice in the qualities of nonattachment of the threefold purity in all ten directions.

Dagpa ta shyi drima mé dzogpé jang chub sem kyé do
I form the resolve toward complete enlightenment, pure and free from defilement of the four extremes.

Deshek jang chub sempa la dagpa sum gyi lü bullo
I offer my body of three purities to the sugatas and bodhisattvas.

Tsé rab drang pé lenam kün dü dé lamé chok tu ngo
I add up all the virtue from every lifetime and dedicate it all to supreme enlightenment.

ix. **Semchen dé dang den gyur chik[s] dugngal kün dang dral war shok[s]**
May all sentient beings possess happiness. May they be free from all misery.[s]

Dé dang tag tu mi dral shying[s] chö kün nyam nyi tokpar shok[s]
May they never be apart from happiness,[s] and may they realize the equality of all things.[s]

x. From: Tulku Urgyen Rinpoche. *Dzogchen Deity Practice*. Translated by Erik Pema Kunsang. (Legget, CA: Rangjung Yeshe Publications, 2016). 21.

Rainbows give us a very good way to understand this. When a rainbow appears in the sky, it doesn't damage the empty sky at all, and yet the rainbow is totally visible. It doesn't change the sky or hurt it in the slightest. It's exactly the same when recognizing the essence of mind, which has been pointed out as being utterly empty. That is the samadhi of suchness. That recognition doesn't have to be left behind in order for cognizance, the samadhi of illumination, to be present; it is spontaneously present by nature. That is true compassion. The sky is the samadhi of suchness, while the rainbow is the samadhi of illumination, the development stage. There is no fight between space and a rainbow, is there? It's exactly like that. First of all, you need to know the samadhi of suchness. Having recognized that, the expression of awareness arises from the essence as the development stage. It is not like construction work. Like the rainbow appearing in the sky, the expression of awareness is the perfect unity of development and completion stages.

Applying this approach is not always possible for every practitioner. The next best way is when you think of one detail at a time, like the head of the deity, the arms, the legs, the body, the attributes, and so forth. Every once in a while, you'll recognize who is visualizing, and again you'll arrive at the state of original empty wakefulness. Then again think of some visualized details, and again recognize, alternating back and forth between the two. That is called the "next best," the medium way of practicing. The least, or minimum, requirement is to first think that everything becomes empty. Recite the mantra OM MAHA SHUNYATA . . . and after that say, "From the state of emptiness, such-and-such appears." In this way, think of one thing at a time, and at the end of the sadhana, again dissolve the whole thing into emptiness. These are three ways to practice development and completion together.

xi. Short Offering and Praise
Hung
Yeshe lhatsok chendren shek
Chinang sangwey chöpa bül
Kusung tuk-yön trinley tö
Bagmey galtrül nyamchag shak
Maha amrita balingta rakta khahi
HUNG
Wisdom deities, I invite you, please come!
I present you outer, inner, and secret offerings.
I praise your body, speech, mind, qualities, and activities
And apologize for my carelessness, mistakes, and breaches!
MAHA AMRITA BALINGTA RAKTA KHAHI

xii. See *Great Accomplishment*. (Legget, CA: Rangjung Yeshe Publications, 2016).

xiii. Tulku Urgyen Rinpoche, unpublished oral commentary.
The practice of a particular yidam deity (*lhag pa'i lha*) contains inconceivable benefit. The yidam should be accomplished with the four nails that combine the vital essence of the deity. These are:
— The nail of the deity samadhi (*ting nge 'dzin lha'i gzer*) refers to the proper visualization of the yidam deity.
— The nail of the essence mantra (*snying po sngags kyi gzer*) refers to the mantra recitation of the yidam deity.
— The key point of the radiating and absorbing (*'phro 'du phrin las kyi gzer*) refers to the nail of the recitation visualization (*dzab dmigs*).
— And finally, but most importantly, the nail of the unchanging wisdom mind (*dgongs pa mi 'gyur ba'i gzer*) refers to the recognition of the essence of your mind.

xiv. See the website of Orgyen Tobgyal Rinpoche: all-otr.org.

xv. Because of weak respect and devotion,⁸ I have gone against the mind of the vajra master.⁸

xvi. Because of lacking affection and modesty,⁸ I have gone against the minds of my dharma brothers and sisters.⁸

xvii. *Lamrim*, Conclusion, page 84: In general, *nyuley* spirits are presented very clearly in the *Kagye* and in the *Lama Gongdü*, as well as in Ratna Lingpa's *Secret Gathering of the Compassionate One*. Yet the specific approach of the Chokling Tersar is as follows.
The twelve *nyuleys* who create obstacles to the practice and wander about meddling at the twelve times of day are given in the original terma in the *Practice Arrangement That Gathers the Entire Intent of the Root Heart Practice*:
(1) The obstructing *nyuleys* who create obstacles at sunset are the *Shatring* daughters cawing like crows; (2) likewise, those who create obstacles in the evening are the *black female robbers*; (3) at nighttime, *the ignorance maintainers*; (4) at midnight, the *ranus* of desire; (5) in the middle of the night, *the duntses* of aversion; (6) at the break of dawn, *the Hedö daughter of the sun*; (7) at sunrise, *White Space Dust*; (8) in the morning, the black female *nagas* and *rakshasas* ; (9) at midday, *the four families of seals of the nagas*; (10) in the late afternoon, *the border terang demons;* (11) in the early afternoon, *the female owners of the land who spread epidemics;* (12) in the early evening, *the maras* and *damsi demons* of samaya-breakers. They are tamed by the twelve messengers who are their antidotes: *Ekadzati, Seyijadra, the Great Red One, Dragon-Faced Dakini, the Great Blazing One, Hundred-Headed She-Wolf, Great She-Crow, Blazing-Mouth Crocodile, Great*

White One, Rakshasi Form, Tsangpa Lingpamo. There are also twelve oppressing substances and mantras.

xviii. To explain these two lines: "The outer elements as the consorts and so forth, meaning also the subjects within which are the sense cognitions—these elements, which are all the spheres of the consorts—are the nonduality of subjects and objects, of means and knowledge." [JOKYAB]

xix. In the context of the syllable BHRUM being the essence of Vairochana, from the seed-syllable HUNG are emanated E YAM RA SUM KEM RAM TI SAM HA BHRUM, through which appear space, wind, the lake of blood, the ground of human flesh, the mountain of skeletons, surrounded by mountains of fire. In addition to these, inside the charnel ground are variegated lotus flowers and the celestial palace. In the case of the peaceful deities, from HRIH appear E YAM BAM LAM BHRUM becoming space, wind, water, earth, Mount Sumeru, and the celestial palace. [JOKYAB]

xx. The base below, the enclosures on the sides, the dome above, the gates, portals, distinctive ornamentation, and so forth include the following: The base beneath, the layered elements, and so forth, the enclosure of the vajra fence and the mountainous flames. To the sides are the ledges and the five-layered walls. As the [ornaments on the walls of the palaces], there are cornices, *mun pa* and *bre phul*, garlands and pendants, and so forth. For roof details there are pillars, beams, pedestals, woodwork, planks, and rooftop. Above these is the dome with eight facets. Above that are the canopy, dharmachakra, and top parasol. In the four directions are the four gates along with their porticos, gateways, and portals. The archways are counted as the sixteen causal and resultant archways, in that the eight causal archways are the two times four sets of steps on the inside and outside of the gate-portal, while the eight resultant archways on the four outer corners of the portals are the *rta rkang*, water-lily, chest, tassel, nose, nozzle, spout, and garuda head—all beautifully arranged in order.

In addition, as ornamentation mentioned from above, there are cornices, garlands, tassels, friezes, and parapets. The embellishments above these are lotus flowers, dharmachakras, jeweled parasols, male and female deer to the right and left sides, as well as top ornaments of vajras and jewels. The decorations on the gates and archways are *glang* lions, portal-wheels, and golden bells resounding the tones of the Three Jewels. To the right and left sides of the four gates are fruit trees and wish-fulfilling trees with tiny bells, groves with auspicious birds, and bathing pools.

On the roof of the palace are parasols, victory banners, pendants, streamers, and tail-fans, as well as many other wonderful décorations.

In the instance of the wrathful palace, there are, moreover, walls of *bhandhas*, pillars of the eight gods, beams of the eight rahulas, pedestals of tortoise, woodwork of the constellation gods, ceilings of human skin, heart top-ornaments, door hangings and banners of human skin, fans of corpse hair, balustrades of backbones, rain spouts of hands, crocodile upper doorsills, tortoise groundsills, entrances of black vipers, and so forth.

These palaces of consecutive peaceful and wrathful [deities] should be ascertained from scaled models, their proportions should be studied, and so forth. [JOKYAB]

xxi. The lotus, sun, haughty spirit, animal, and so forth, in the case of the wrathful. The haughty spirits, *drekpa*, are the guardians of the directions, and the types belonging to rahula, naga, gyalpo, and senmo. *The Magical Net, Mayajala*, system mentions bull, buffalo, leopard, tiger, and bear. In addition to these, the *Eight Sadhana Teachings, Kabgye,* adds garuda, snake, and lion to make the eight main animals. [JOKYAB]

xxii. For instance, the lion throne symbolizes matchless might, the lotus nonattachment, the sun and moon symbolize bliss and emptiness. [DILGO KHYENTSE]

For information regarding video and audio recordings, published teachings, and programs in the lineage of Chokling Tersar, please access one of the following websites:

www.lotustreasure.com

www.rangjung.com
Rangjung Yeshe Publications and Translations

www.shedrub.org
Shedrub Development Mandala

www.tsoknyirinpoche.org
Tsoknyi Rinpoche Activities and Teachings

www.CGLF.org
Chokgyur Lingpa Foundation

www.gomde.dk
Rangjung Yeshe Gomde, Denmark

www.erikpemakunsang.com
Works of Erik Pema Kunsang

www.all-otr.org
Teachings of Orgyen Tobgyal Rinpoche

www.ingramcontent.com/pod-product-compliance
Lightning Source LLC
Chambersburg PA
CBHW020329170426
43200CB00006B/317